TUGS AND TOWING BARGES
ON THE
HUMBER
WATERWAYS

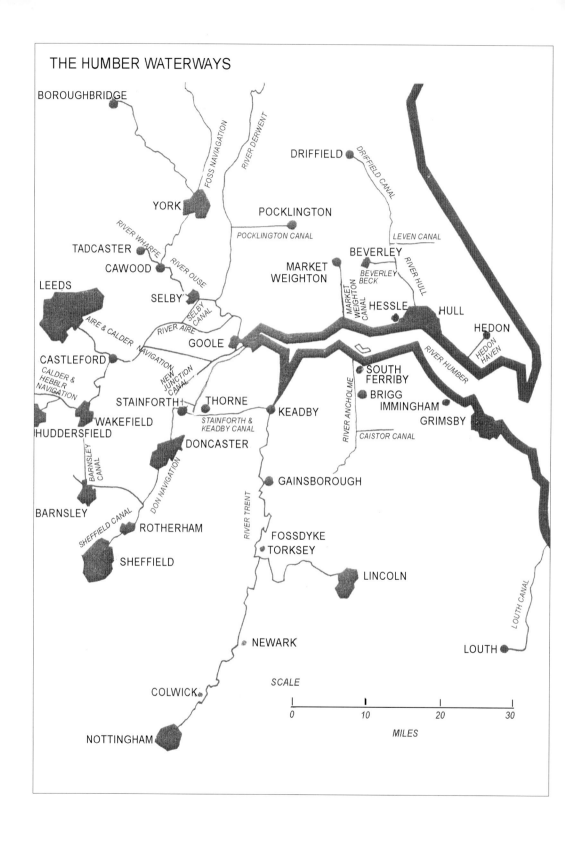

THE HUMBER WATERWAYS

TUGS AND TOWING BARGES ON THE
HUMBER WATERWAYS

MIKE TAYLOR

TEMPUS

Frontispiece: Map of the Humber Inland Waterways. (John Bryce)

First published 2006

Tempus Publishing Limited
The Mill, Brimscombe Port,
Stroud, Gloucestershire, GL5 2QG
www.tempus-publishing.com

British Library Cataloguing in Publication Data.
A catalogue record for this book is available from the British Library.

ISBN 0 7524 3804 2

Typesetting and origination by Tempus Publishing Limited.
Printed in Great Britain.

Contents

Acknowledgements

Douglas Carey, Henry Dawson, Lawrie Dews, George Trevethick and Jarvis Whitton, as well as several now-deceased boatmen, have provided much of the information used in this book. Numerous individuals, newspapers, companies and public bodies have kindly allowed me to use their photographs.

Books by Mike Taylor, published by Tempus:

The Calder and Hebble Navigation, 2002
The River Trent Navigation, 2000
The Sheffield and South Yorkshire Navigation, 2001
Shipping on the Humber (North Bank), 2003
Shipping on the Humber (South Bank), 2003
The Yorkshire Ouse Navigation, 2002

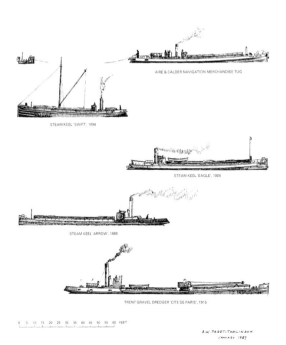

Edward Paget-Tomlinson's drawings of some steam towing barges of the Humber waterways, are shown together with their years of build. *Swift*, with a hull of Low Moor iron – which did not rust, though tended to crack – was built for the Farmers' Co. of Barton-on-Humber; *Eagle* was constructed of steel for Rishworth, Ingleby & Lofthouse, the Hull millers; Henry Leetham & Sons, the York millers, owned the iron *Arrow* and the steel *Cité de Paris* was built in the First World War as an ammunition carrier but spent most of its working life under the ownership of Lincoln & Hull Water Transport.

Introduction

The role of tugs and towing barges seems to have been neglected in the limited amount of material published on the Humber's inland waterways. This book attempts to fill that gap.

Paddle tugs were the norm in the nineteenth century, having the advantage of easy operation in shallow water, but by the start of the twentieth century, screw tugs, with their much more compact engine layout, were being developed to work under these conditions.

Prior to the 1930s, almost all cargo-carrying craft on the Humber waterways were towed by tugs for some part of their working lives. Lighters were towed between the docks and river Hull and keels and sloops often used public towing services to reach Goole, Keadby, Torksey and York from Hull before, perhaps, seeking a further tow to Doncaster, Lincoln, Leeds or Wakefield.

Steam-powered tugs and towing barges were gradually superseded by or converted into diesel-engined units from the late 1920s onwards. Also, in the mid-1930s, diesel engines began to be fitted to new barges and installed in craft that formerly sailed. The powered vessels thus produced were then able to tow the remaining dumb craft. Motor-dumb pairs were prevalent, especially between the mid-1930s and 1950s, leading to a marked fall in demand for tugs.

The various Humber waterways, strangely categorised in canal circles as the 'north-eastern waterways', each had a different towing scenario until nationalisation in 1948 and some characteristic features persisted until well after this time. These are described in the early chapters of this book and illustrated using photographs, mainly from the twentieth century, none of which have appeared in my other Tempus books. Some of the maps included here have, however, been used in these volumes.

To the layman, 'push' and 'tug' must seem to be contradictory terms but, after trials on the Thames in 1948, E.C. Jones & Son of Brentford introduced their 'Bantam' push tugs in 1951. Several advantages were claimed for push-towing over pull-towing, including a 40 per cent increase in fuel efficiency and the need for less manpower to handle a tow because, whereas all craft in a pull tow usually had to have a man at the helm of each vessel, only a tug crew is necessary in a push tow where tug and barges act as a rigid unit held tightly together by wire ropes. Many operators subsequently changed over to push-towing and this is still prevalent around the Humber, being featured in Chapter Seven.

Illustrations showing craft owned by most major carrying companies in the region have been selected. Each photograph is credited individually, apart from those taken by me or selected from my own collection, which are uncredited. I have also interspersed some recollections of men who worked on the waterways amongst the illustrations.

Mike Taylor

Notes

'Dumb' is used to describe a vessel without an engine.

The First and Second World Wars are often quoted by boatmen and others when asked to date an event. I have also used these terms in captions and, for completeness sake, it should be stated that they refer to 1914–18 and 1939–45 respectively.

The following abbreviations have been used:

A&CNC	Aire & Calder Navigation Co.
BOCM	British Oil & Cake Mills
BTC	British Transport Commission
BWB	British Waterways Board (currently British Waterways)
C&HN	Calder & Hebble Navigation
D&IWE	Docks & Inland Waterways Executive
G&HSTC	Goole & Hull Steam Towing Company
L&LC	Leeds & Liverpool Canal
RIL	Rishworth, Ingleby & Lofthouse (subsequently Spillers)
S&SYNC	Sheffield & South Yorkshire Navigation Co.
TNC	Trent Navigation Co.
UTC	United Towing Co.
YDDC	Yorkshire Dry Dock Co.

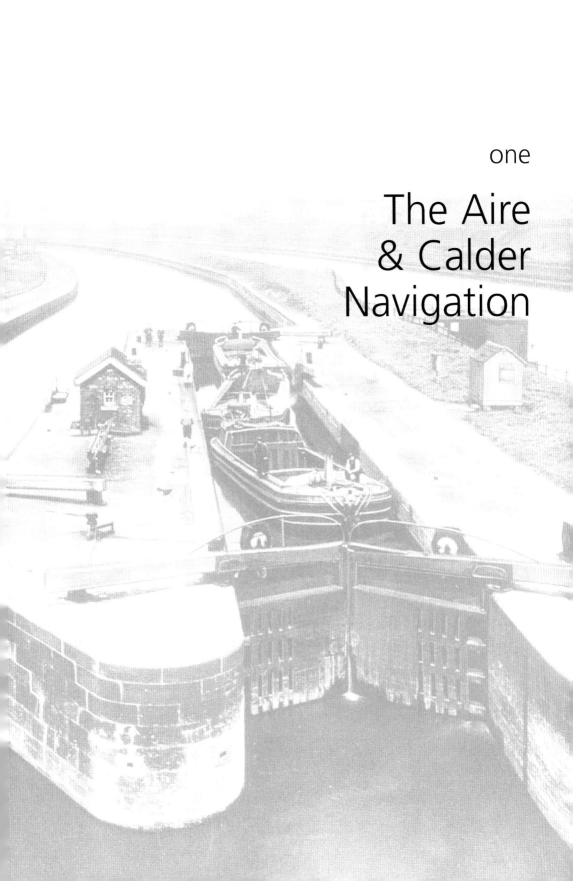

one

The Aire
& Calder
Navigation

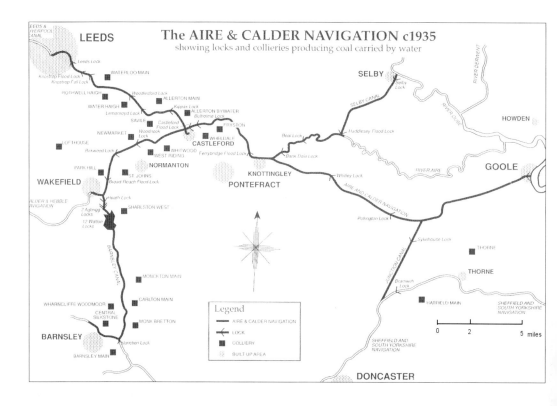

The AIRE & CALDER NAVIGATION c1935
showing locks and collieries producing coal carried by water

COMPARTMENT BOATS (TOM PUDDINGS)

Inextricably linked with the A&CN was the compartment boat or Tom Pudding operation whereby up to 40 tons of coal was loaded at various West Riding Colliery staithes into 20ft x 15ft iron pans having a depth of 9ft. These were then assembled into trains to be towed to Goole by steam tugs where their cargoes were tipped individually by one of five distinctive hydraulically powered hoists on the dock estate into the holds of sea-going vessels for delivery either to near-European or English south and east coast ports, including some on the river Thames. The system, devised by the A&CNC's engineer, later general manager, W.H. Bartholomew, as a response to encroaching railway services, began in the 1860s and continued for over one and a quarter centuries. Originally the compartments (pans) were push-towed in steerable trains of up to twelve units but were pull-towed from about 1900. Most of the 48ft x 15ft steam tugs were built in the late nineteenth century by Thomas Scott & Co. at Goole.

During their lifetime, 55 million tons were carried by the puddings, usually in 19-pan trains on the A&CN. These could pass unbroken through Bulholme lock and those below. It was difficult to find return cargoes from Goole but, especially before and after the First World War, wool, wire, timber, metal ores and oil seeds were carried up to Wakefield and Leeds.

During the late 1950s, diesel tugs replaced the steam tugs. The demand for coal fell in the 1960s, when natural gas began to replace coal gas as a domestic and industrial fuel, and smokeless fuel, loaded at Doncaster and Castleford, began to be carried in 1967, completely replacing coal by the early 1970s. The final cargo was delivered by the puddings in April 1986.

Steam compartment tug *No. 12* is heading past No. 5 Swing Bridge at Goole with a train of loaded pans in the 1930s. The jebus, or leader, is in use to lift the leading pan and deflect the tug's wash beneath and to the sides of the tow. During the Second World War, the bridge shown was locked overnight, causing delays of up to three hours when it was reopened at 6 a.m. (Hull Maritime Museum)

Above: Steam compartment tug *No. 14* on the A&CN at Methley Bridge delivering empty pans to colliery staithes on the Wakefield Branch in the 1920s. The jebus is not needed with a train of light pans and is pushed in front of the tug.

A steam compartment tug hauling its train out of Bulholme lock in the 1900s, bound for Goole.

Right: After nationalisation in 1948, the D&IWE fitted wheelboxes and chose to give colliery names to some of the steam compartment tugs and here *Highgate*, strangely named after a colliery with no waterway access, hauls a loaded train past Ferrybridge A Power Station in the early 1950s with the jebus serving its purpose. (BWB)

Opposite below: A steam compartment tug hauls loaded puddings down Castleford Cut towards Bulholme lock in the 1940s. The walkway formed along one side of the train gives the tug's crew access to all the pans, if necessary.

Above: In the mid-1950s, the unique floating hoist (No.4) was overhauled in Goole South Dock's dry dock, close to where it was built in 1908. It is shown being hauled across the dock by four steam compartment tugs to its position opposite No.5 hoist, also visible. No.4 hoist's tipping days ended in 1967. (Norman Burnitt)

Left: The coaster *Humbergate* loading at No.5 hoist in Goole's South Dock during the early 1950s. A tipped pan is visible on the apparatus. The final cargo carried by the puddings was transhipped here in April 1986.

Just before Easter 1958, steam pudding tug *No. 14* came rushing beneath Rawcliffe Bridge, near Goole, much faster than usual, to be confronted by a breach in the bank separating the canal from the Dutch River. The tow was sucked into the broken bank, partially damming it, as shown, but repairs were made over the Easter holiday and the waterway opened for traffic as usual immediately afterwards. (Stan Barrass)

The 1889-built steam compartment tug *No. 6* was fitted with a 126hp diesel engine and refurbished to include new steel decking in 1956. It was renamed *Waterloo* and is seen on trials which resulted in orders being placed for seven new diesel tugs. (Norman Burnitt)

Above: One of the seven diesel compartment tugs, built in the late 1950s, hauling a train from Doncaster to Goole in 1980. *Allerton Bywater*, *Water Haigh* and *Wheldale* were built by E.C. Jones of Brentford; *Brodsworth*, *Kellingley* and *West Riding* came from Dunstons at Thorne and *Hatfield* was a product of Camplings of Goole. All were fitted with 135hp diesel engines.

Merchandise Tows

In 1831, the A&CNC introduced a towage service to move their own craft over their waterway. In 1857, well before the compartment boats were introduced, this service was extended to include by-traders' craft and described by the company as a 'General Merchandise Tow'. Towage was by steam tug or steam towing barge and, until the 1940s, there were daily services between Goole and Leeds and Goole and Wakefield with tugs going out from Goole's Barge Dock early one day and returning late the next. At the height of its popularity in the 1920s, the services were duplicated with overnight runnings.

Before nationalisation in January 1948, the A&CNC were planning to replace the remaining steam merchandise tugs (*No. 7*, *No. 8* and the less powerful *No. 2*) with diesel towing barges. *Beta* and *Gamma* appeared later that year and worked between Hull and Leeds or Wakefield, obviating the need for towage of their dumb craft on the tidal waters between Goole and Hull which hitherto had been performed by the Goole & Hull Steam Towing Co.

Right: One of the A&CNC's four 85ft x 15ft steam towing barges, and three of its four-man crew pose for the camera. The craft carried very few cargoes in the twentieth century.

Opposite below: The 1900-built No.3 hoist in Goole's Aldam Dock acted as reserve to No.5 hoist at busy times during the final few years of operation of the puddings. *Sybille* is loading smokeless fuel for Scandinavia here in 1983, with *Wheldale* in attendance as shunt tug.

With its crew aboard, merchandise towing barge tug *No. 12*, built in 1891 by Thomas Scott & Co., is moored near Goole's Lowther Bridge. Compartment hoist No.2 lies beyond in Ouse Dock.

A merchandise towing barge heading down the river Calder from Wakefield towards Castleford in the 1920s with six craft in tow and Methley Railway Bridge in the background. Eight tugs and towing barges were in service at this time.

A 1929 view at Fryston, below Castleford, from the third vessel in a merchandise tow behind a towing barge heading up the A&CN. (G.H. Holgate)

A towing barge, tug *No.11*, entering the '5-mile pond' between Ferrybridge flood lock and Castleford with a tow in 1931. (Ron Gosney Collection)

AIRE AND CALDER NAVIGATION.

CAUTION TO NAVIGATION TUGMEN.

THE NAVIGATION HAVE RECEIVED COMPLAINTS THAT DENSE SMOKE IS EMITTED FROM THEIR TUGS WHEN PASSING ALONG THE NAVIGATION (ESPECIALLY THROUGH BROTHERTON AND KNOTTINGLEY.)

THE ATTENTION OF ENGINEERS AND FIREMEN HAS ALREADY BEEN CALLED TO THE FACT THAT WHAT IS COMPLAINED OF CAN BE AVOIDED BY CAREFUL FIRING AND THE PROPER USE OF THE STEAM JET.

NOTICE IS HEREBY GIVEN THAT INSPECTORS WILL BE APPOINTED TO MAKE OBSERVATIONS AND THAT IN ALL CASES WHERE SUFFICIENT EVIDENCE IS OBTAINED LEGAL PROCEEDINGS WILL BE TAKEN AGAINST THE PERSON RESPONSIBLE.

BY ORDER.

LEEDS. JULY, 1914.

392—1914.

N.B.—This Circular to be preserved by the person to whom it is handed and produced when required by an official of the Navigation.

With Knottingley passed but Brotherton still ahead, the crew of tug *No. 11* in the previous photograph will have to continue to heed the warning in this notice as they head upriver to Castleford. (Ron Gosney Collection)

Merchandise tug *No. 8* and its Goole-bound tow of light vessels in Pollington lock in the early 1930s. The A&CNC's merchandise tugs, with dimensions 62ft x 15ft, were longer than the compartment tugs.

A poorly patronised merchandise tow heading west from Goole to either Leeds or Wakefield having just passed King's Mill, Knottingley.

Stan Barrass, merchandise tug skipper in the 1930s

Goole's Barge Dock always held craft waiting for a tow up the canal. Many had loaded at Hull and come upriver behind one of the Goole & Hull Steam Towing Co.'s steam tugs. Others had loaded at Goole. The Aire & Calder tugs lay overnight in Barge Dock and the fireman began to liven up the fire in the early hours ready for a 4 a.m. departure. As steam pressure was rising, the tugmaster would arrive with a list of vessels he had collected from the A&CNC offices the previous evening. Each barge captain who had booked on the tow was hailed from the dockside and told of his position in the line. Heavier the cargo, nearer the tug was the rule and this always worried owners of heavily laden old wooden craft that would then have their timbers flexed by pulls fore and aft for the next few hours.

As soon as the mate and engineer had arrived to complete the tug's four-man crew, the train was assembled, the tug's funnel lowered to pass under the bridge and the 'Leedser' set off, with barges strung out at thirty-yard intervals. The tugmaster stood comfortably warm behind his shelter plate but, on each barge, one of the two-man crew stood clutching the tiller on an open deck, huddled well down inside his top coat with only a flimsy weatherboard for protection against the elements. The tug crew worked 'spells' throughout the voyage with the tugmaster and mate taking turns at the helm and the engineer and fireman sharing duties behind the two control levers on deck, periodically going down into the engine room to tend to the fire.

Several Tom Pudding trains would be met and, just when you thought there would be a collision, their tug captains flicked their rear compartments out of the way as we passed.

At the locks, the tug crew worked one side and the lockkeeper the other. When the river section was reached after Ferrybridge, the 'down' Leedser was usually met heading for Goole, towed coal barges heading down to the power station or bound for York were passed, barges were always entering and leaving Fryston and Wheldale basins and we were always delayed if any of these happened to be pulled by a horse. Bulholme lock was the busiest on the whole waterway but, once through and along Castleford Cut to four-lane-ends, some craft were dropped off to make their own way down to Castleford wharves.

Coal was everywhere from here up to Leeds, with lots of other traffic to delay us at the locks and, if we had more than five vessels left in the tow, three pennings were needed at each of the four shorter locks we had to pass through before reaching Leeds, with the second and third groups having to be pulled through by hand.

Arrival at Leeds took place between 5 p.m. and 10 p.m. The crew then had to barrow coal aboard, prepare themselves some food and unroll their mattresses to bed down for a few hours sleep before another 4 a.m. start on the voyage back to Goole in the morning.

Above: The steam-powered merchandise tows finished about the time of nationalisation in 1948. The 76ft x 15\'bdft diesel towing barge *Beta*, one of four built by Harkers at Knottingley in 1949 for the D&IWE to carry cargoes and pull the few remaining dumb craft requiring a tow, is shown moored at Pollington in the early 1950s with the dumb barge that it was towing. (Stan Barrass)

Right: In the early 1970s, when BWB had almost ceased to pull-tow conventional barges, *Kappa B W*, one of the four craft built by Harkers, was lengthened from its original 76ft to 110ft, thereby increasing its carrying capacity. The barge is shown at Pollington, heading solo up the A&CN. (BWB)

Other West Riding Pull Tows

The A&CN was a steam-tug waterway for the first half of the twentieth century. As well as the A&CNC's compartment tugs and merchandise tugs, large canal carriers had their own tugs which were busy well into the 1950s hauling coal barges, especially around Leeds. Hunts' *Emma* hauled many owners' unpowered craft through the city on the towpath-less stretch of the river Aire between Leeds lock and the L&LC's entrance lock. Duttons, Hargreaves, Leeds Corporation Electricity Dapartment (LCED) and Leeds Industrial Co-operative Society (LICS) were major carriers of coal and both moored their loaded craft in Leeds Dock or 'tatie basin' off the main line of the navigation, just above Leeds lock, when waiting for discharge berths. LCED began with a small power station on the river Aire at Whitehall Road, reached from the A&CN via an arm of the L&LC, but opened much more substantial premises at Kirkstall in 1931 and had a new canal loop built here, together with six new motor barges and several dumb craft to deliver coal 3½ miles and six locks up the L&LC to it.

Also, in the 1930s, Harkers' tugs handled petrol deliveries to Castleford, Leeds and Wakefield, both RIL's (later Spillers') and LICS's steam keels brought flour to Leeds from Hull, and Branfords carried sand to Knottingley glassmakers. Tom Fletcher delivered imported wood-pulp for Barnsley paper mills from Hull to Wakefield and the Calder Carrying Co.'s and Hunts' towing barges handled their owners' general cargo dumb barges.

Some owners had new motor tugs built in the 1950s to replace their steam tugs, but most of these were phased out in the 1960s.

The former A&CNC steam tug *Emma*, owned by John Hunt & Sons (Leeds) passes craft moored outside Leeds Terminus on the towpath-less stretch of the river Aire, along which it towed dumb craft several times each day. Boat horses were tramped through Leeds via The Calls and past Spillers' large warehouse, seen to the left of the view.

Leeds Industrial Cooperative Society began retailing domestic coal from their Victoria Wharf in the city in 1880, using a large fleet of horse-drawn craft to bring the fuel from West Riding collieries. They hired a steam tug in 1918, purchased the steam tug *Unity* in 1921 and had a motor towing barge, *Albion*, built by Scarrs of Hessle in 1936. *Albion* is shown hauling two coal-laden craft into Leeds lock in the 1970s.

LICS's diesel tug *The President*, built in 1958 by Dunstons of Thorne, leaving Leeds lock in the 1970s with a couple of loaded coal boats in tow. The distant pair of lock gates was added to turn the original small Leeds lock, shown by the two pairs of gates nearer the camera, into one of much greater capacity.

LICS's towing barge *Albion* and diesel tug *The President* moored at the company's Victoria Wharf in Leeds along with two loaded dumb coal barges in the 1960s. The wharf was situated on the river Aire, off the A&CN. This traffic ended in 1975.

The steam tug *Aire*, built in 1902 by Henry Scarr of Hessle and purchased by Hargreaves in 1919 to replace horse-haulage, towing craft on Knostrop Cut in the 1940s. (Doug Walker Collection)

Hargreaves' steam tug *Audrey*, acquired in 1940, hauling one of their 1950s-built, 200-ton capacity dumb barges after its cargo has been discharged at Ferrybridge A Power Station.

Hargreaves' diesel-engined towing barge *Lawson*, built for them by Dunstons of Thorne in 1942, lies moored outside the company's Castleford yard. The vessel occasionally helped LCED with deliveries to Kirkstall Power Station. (Hargreaves)

Lawson in 1979, renamed *Viking* and owned by Viking Commercial Services, delivers a pilot to the coaster *Lisa* which has just left the Dutch River at Goole to head down the Ouse and out to sea. Occasionally *Viking* also acted as a tug in the port.

Hargreaves' motor tug *Else Margareta*, built at Hull in 1958 by the YDDC, gives guests a short trip on the river Aire after its naming ceremony at Ferrybridge. The vessel was sold in 1961 as the company changed over from tug-hauled dumb craft to motor barges. (Hargreaves)

LCED's *Arc*, built by Dunstons of Thorne, posed in the 1930s on the Redcote loop of the L&LC at Kirkstall power station with its towing hook visible behind the helmsman. Two dumb barges were hauled by these motor towing barges on the A&CN parts of their voyages to collect coal, but the three units were worked singly on the L&LC, the dumb craft often pulled by horse.

A LCED three-barge unit penning through Knostrop Fall lock on the A&CN in the 1930s, heading for a colliery to load. The original course of the river Aire lies to the left of the view with the twentieth-century alteration to the right.

Hunts' steam towing barge *Hunt's Brent* heading west on the A&CN near New Bridge, bound for Leeds in 1936 with a dumb barge in tow, an hour or so after leaving Goole. The vessel was built by Scarrs of Hessle in 1930 and, after conversion to a motor barge and sale to coal merchants, was renamed *Lindsy* in 1951. (Humberside Libraries)

Branfords' *Lyric* towing their dumb barge *Joe* up the A&CN loaded with glassmaking sand for Knottingley in 1965. Both vessels were 1899-built, ex-A&CNC merchandise towing barges with their steam plant removed. At the time, *Lyric*, which carried 135 tons, was fitted with a Gardner diesel engine to drive a huge propellor. (John Branford)

The Calder Carrying Co.'s wooden towing barge *Frank W.*, built at Mirfield in the mid-1930s and powered by a large 40hp Bolinder engine, ice-breaking on the C&HN below Copley Bridge, near Sowerby Bridge, in 1947. (Bill Carey Collection)

T. Fletcher & Sons' steam packet *Queensview*, built at Goole for service in the First World War, is shown here discharging wire at Wakefield in the 1940s. During the late 1920s and 1930s, the company brought large amounts of Finnish wood-pulp, imported via Hull, to Heath entrance lock where it was transhipped to smaller horse-drawn craft for carriage along the Barnsley Canal to Barnsley paper mills.

Above: Harkers' 70ft x 15ft diesel tug *Lion*, built by them at Knottingley in 1931, was designed with accommodation for crews of the petrol tankers it towed who were not allowed to live aboard their own craft. It was shortened to 57ft and the extra accommodation removed in 1943. The tug was sold in 1956. (Harkers)

Right: James W. Cook's *Kittiwake C* tows their dumb barge *Auk C* into Bulholme lock in the early 1960s, bound for Leeds. This long lock allows a 19-pan compartment boat train to pen through unbroken with conventional craft fitted into the embayment.

Opposite below: During the Second World War, a shortage of tugs led to Harkers using the pudding tugs and UTC's *Seeker* to haul their dumb tankers up to Leeds. The 58ft x 15ft steam tug *Elsa Partiss*, shown travelling solo on the Humber, was built by Warrens of New Holland in 1908 and purchased by Harkers for the purpose in 1947. (Hull Maritime Museum)

Taken half an hour after the previous photograph, *Kittiwake C* and *Auk C* enter the river Aire at four-lane-ends above Castleford flood lock en route for Leeds. The helmsman's scant protection from the elements provided by the weatherboard is clearly shown.

Flixborough Shipping's motor barge *Olive Pittwood* towing their dumb barge *Mallyan* on the A&CN at Stanley Ferry. Due to a post-war shortage of engines, both craft had been left dumb after being built by Dunstons in 1953, but one had been found for the towing barge by the time of this 1957 photograph. The vessels are carrying coal for Scunthorpe steelworks loaded at Parkhill Colliery staithe, a mile further up the canal, and would be bound via Goole for Flixborough Wharf on the Trent. (BWB)

The diesel-engined former compartment tug *Wheldale*, after its sale by BWB, towing the effluent carrier *Trentcal* down to Goole as it leaves Lemonroyd lock on the Leeds Branch in 1987. The tanker was being re-engined at the time. The effluent traffic ceased in 1997. (Andy Horn)

two

The Yorkshire Ouse Navigation

At the start of the twentieth century there were three towing businesses based in York. Henry Leetham & Sons, the millers, and T.F. Wood & Co., wharfingers, operated towing barges to pull their own craft. By 1920, the City Corporation, who owned the navigation, also owned five tugs which had provided a public towing service between York and Hull, Goole and Selby since 1879. The City of York's tugs were *Ebor Express* (1878–1930), *City of York* (1888–1923), *Lancelot* (1905–1947), *Sir Joseph Rymer* (1909–1937) and *Robie* (1915–1924). Many York-bound cargoes of West Riding coal came to Selby via the A&CN and Selby Canal and were hauled to their destination from here by these tugs. Woods did extensive work for Rowntrees, the York-based chocolate manufacturer, delivering often exotic and valuable cargoes to their wharf and warehouse off the river Foss with the Ouse bringing three or four barges twice a week from Hull or Goole. They had another towing barge, *Brunton*, built at Beverley in 1934 and were then delivering, in addition to other chocolate-making ingredients, about 800 tons of sugar per week to Rowntrees, as well as goods for other customers.

Until 1924, when their preferential rates were withdrawn, Leethams were responsible for five sixths of York's barge traffic. The company and its craft were taken over by Spillers in 1928.

In the 1920s, large mills which extracted oil from seeds were built at Barlby, just above Selby. Raw materials were imported via Hull and delivered by water in the mill company's dumb barges, hauled by tugs owned by Whitakers of Hull, but, eventually, with some haulage by their own tugs.

Akesters of Hull used their towing barges and dumb craft to deliver grain from Hull to Kirby's flour mill at Selby from the 1920s to the 1960s.

The activities of the Goole & Hull Steam Towing Co. were at their height throughout the early decades of the twentieth century, providing a public towing service for inland waterway craft between the two ports. Almost all vessels loading at Hull for wharves on the A&CN came to Goole by use of this service. The company also did some coastal work with sea-going lighters, trading regularly as far as the river Thames.

All the tugs and towing barges on the Ouse were coal-fired and steam-driven until the Selby mills acquired an oil-fired steam tug, *Oco*, in 1947. Diesel power began to replace steam after Whitakers converted their *Cawood* in 1953.

The towing services based at York, Selby and Goole were in gradual decline during the century and were all phased out after the Second World War. After becoming part of BOCM in 1952, a decision was made to replace the Selby oil mills fleet of dumb craft by self-propelled motor barges, and regular pull-towing on the Ouse then died out.

Opposite above: A map showing the Yorkshire Ouse and A&CN.

Opposite below: Blundy, Clark & Co.'s motor barge *Catherine Clark*, not built as a towing barge but often used to pull a dumb barge for convenience, dredges sand from the river Swale, near Boroughbridge in the 1980s.

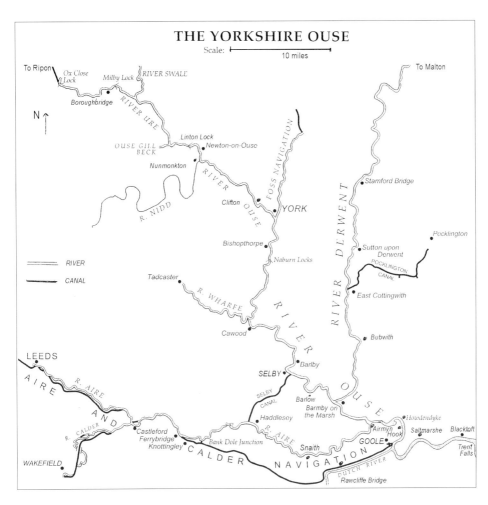

THE YORKSHIRE OUSE

Scale: |⊢————————| 10 miles

To Ripon • Ox Close Lock • Milby Lock • RIVER SWALE
• Boroughbridge
RIVER URE
To Malton

N ↑

Linton Lock
OUSE GILL BECK • Newton-on-Ouse

Nunmonkton

R. NIDD

RIVER OUSE

FOSS NAVIGATION

Clifton • YORK

RIVER DERWENT

• Stamford Bridge

• Pocklington

• Bishopthorpe

Naburn Locks

• Sutton upon Derwent
POCKLINGTON CANAL

————— RIVER
━━━━━ CANAL

Tadcaster •

R. WHARFE

• East Cottingwith

Cawood •

• Bubwith

LEEDS •

R. AIRE

AIRE AND

Barlby
SELBY •
SELBY CANAL

OUSE

R. CALDER

Castleford
Ferrybridge •
Knottingley

Bank Dole Junction

Haddlesey •

Barlow
Barmby on the Marsh

R. AIRE

Snaith

Airmyn
Hook

Howdendyke •
Saltmarshe • Blacktoft

GOOLE •

Trent Falls

WAKEFIELD •

CALDER NAVIGATION

DUTCH RIVER
Rawcliffe Bridge

Above: Blundy, Clark & Co.'s diesel towing barge *Doris Clark* was built in 1924 by the Goole Shipbuilding & Repairing Co. and fitted with a Kromhout engine. The vessel, shown here on a picture extracted from the engine manufacturer's catalogue, was sold to the Direct Delivery Service in 1956 and renamed *Delivery*. (Ron Cowl Collection)

Woods' steam towing barge *Ouse*, built in 1890 by Watsons of Gainsborough, heads up the river Ouse on the outskirts of York in the 1940s with two loaded barges in tow. The vessel itself could carry 60 tons and was moored at Woods' own wharf on Queen's staithe over weekends where it was bunkered with its weekly requirement of 25 tons of coal.

Opposite below: Anglo-American Oil's towing tanker barge *Fossgate* and dumb tanker *Lowgate*, both built in 1925 by Henry Scarr at Hessle, worked regularly up the Ouse to the company's depot on the Foss at York. They are shown moored on that river having just delivered 60 tons and 70 tons of petrol respectively. (Dunstons)

From a postcard used in 1914, *Yendis*, one of Leethams' steam towing barges, heads down the Ouse through the wooden 1792-built toll bridge at Selby (replaced by a steel structure in 1970). The vessel illustrates an Ouse tradition of naming craft by reversing the spellings of other names, e.g. *Mahteel*, *Semloh*, *Reklaw* and so on.

Opposite below: On a picture postcard used in 1909, York Corporation's steam tug *Lancelot* is heading upriver at Selby, with the toll bridge in the background at the start of the 120-degree bend in the river. This tug handled the final Corporation tows to York, being sold in 1947 to Foster Tow of Hull, though it worked mainly between Hull and Selby in the 1930s and 1940s.

Above: Lawrie Dews, who spent his entire working life aboard craft on the Ouse, identified this steam towing barge athwart Selby Toll Bridge, the Ouse's biggest hazard to navigation, as Akesters' coal-fired *Mary & Agnes* which regularly towed a couple of wooden dumb craft from Hull to Kirby's Selby flour mill in the 1920s.

The River Ouse, Selby.

THE RIVER OUSE SELBY

15

Lawrie Dews, Selby mills tows to Hull and back in the 1930s

Dad's barge had first to be dropped down stern-first trailing the anchor from the oil mills, through both bridges to the (York) Corporation pier where the tug, usually *Robie*, picked us up along with three other barges and towed us downriver in two lines.

At Hull, if we were loading at Alexandra or King George Dock, the tug would throw our rope off outside the dock and go back to moor overnight at Victoria pier ready to take four loaded barges back to Selby next morning. We would moor outside the dock entrance lock and pole ourselves into it when the gates opened. When the lock had been filled, the lock gateman came round for the two shillings we had to give him for penning us up before tide-time. Then, one of the men aboard would use a cog boat and scull across the dock with a line to fasten to something suitable such as a ship, barge or bollard, so that we could heave ourselves across the dock using our warping rollers and tie up for the night. The oil mills didn't provide us with coal for our fires and the sea-going tugs' full bunkers were a great temptation when their crews were absent.

After loading seeds for crushing from ships, often by the rip and tip method through a chute after weighing, we were usually ordered to set off for Selby on the next tide and if it was tide-time early next morning, we'd pole ourselves to the lock the previous evening to make sure that we got into the first penning. Five hours before high water, the top gates were opened and the barges were heaved and pushed into the lock. Four hours before high water, the top gates were closed, the lock gateman blew his whistle and the lock would be run off. When the bottom gates opened *Robie* or sometimes *Lancelot* would come astern into the lock and the mate would throw us a heaving line. Our ten-inch tow rope would be fastened to this, pulled aboard the tug and put onto the port or starboard towing hook. Another barge would hang onto us and two other barges would be fastened similarly onto the other hook. The captains and mates then took it in turn to hang onto the wooden tiller during the usual six-hour run to Selby on the incoming tide. The two lines were reduced to single file to pass through Selby's bridges.

Approaching the bridges, the tug gave one long and six short blasts as it had previously also done at Hook Railway Bridge, Boothferry Bridge and Barmby Railway Bridge. With luck, the bridge signal, which looked like a pair of spectacles, would drop to indicate that both the road and railway bridges were swinging. If not, the tug would have to turn the tow head-to-tide to hold its barges in the current, wait for the signal and then turn again to pull them through the bridges. As the fourth barge rounded the bend and the mills came into view, the tug's towing hook would be hammered to release the tow and the other barges would let go of each other. The barges would steer into the bank to turn into the tidal flow, allowing them to use their anchors and the tide to reach their moorings.

Opposite above: York City Corporation sold the coal-fired steam tug *Robie*, built in 1915 by Henry Scarr at Hessle, to Selby oil mills in 1924 and the vessel has turned in the river between the road and rail swing bridges to bring its tow to a halt, probably because the road (toll) bridge has remained closed to river traffic. The dumb barge, *Selby Pollux*, would be bound for the oil mills at Barlby and, judging by the rope trailing from this vessel, the next barge in the tow would probably have hung onto the rail bridge.

Opposite below: In the 1950s, when this aerial view of Goole was taken, the oil mills at Selby and its craft had been taken over by BOCM and their tug *Robie* is heading upriver past the port's Victoria Lock with four lighters in tow, loaded with seeds for crushing from ships in Hull docks.

Designed to redress a shortage of small tugs during the Second World War, TID (Tugs in Defence?) tugs were built, chiefly by Dunstons of Thorne, at a rate of one per week by welding together parts delivered by road from several land-based fabricators. This view of the Thorne yard shows a steam tug in the water, two craft under construction and A&CN compartment boats in use to store steam boilers for the tugs.

This picture from the Richard Dunston catalogue shows one of the TID units being delivered to the boatyard by lorry in the 1940s. (Dunstons)

With *Robie* ready for scrapping, the oil mills bought the oil-fired *Tid-118* in 1947 and renamed it *Oco* (an abbreviation of Olympia Cake and Oil Mills). The tug is shown heading upriver to Barlby, past part of its owners' fleet of dumb barges in the 1950s. (Fred Harland)

Left: In 1950, the oil mills purchased another TID, the coal-fired *Tid-77*, which they renamed *Ardol* after one of the mill products. The vessel is shown heading down to Cochranes, the Selby shipbuilders, in the 1950s to attend the launch of a new trawler. (Ron Cowl)

Below: In 1961, *Oco* collided with a ship and sank at Swinefleet on the lower Ouse with the loss of two crew members. It was raised, renamed *Selby Olympia* and is shown here at Barlby on a snowy day in early 1963 as it neared the end of its working life with BOCM. (H.M. Lobley)

BOCM had eighteen self-propelled diesel barges built by Dunstons of Thorne between 1952 and 1963. This view, from one of the earliest of these vessels, *Selby Michael*, shows an older dumb craft, *Selby Cygnus*, under tow downriver above Goole during the period of transition of their fleet from dumb to power. Boothferry Bridge and the newer M62 crossing may be seen in the background.(Lawrie Dews Collection)

By the 1960s, Akesters' steam towing barge and the wooden barges that it towed (see page 41) had been replaced by the diesel-engined *Windyridge* and steel dumb craft, shown in 1960 at Barmby Railway Swing Bridge whilst returning from Selby to Hull. River levels were low at the time so there was no need to swing the bridge.

The Goole & Hull Steam Towing Co.'s tug *Goole No.3*, built at South Shields by J.P. Rennolds & Sons in 1899, running free on the Humber in the 1920s. The vessel was broken up in 1930. (Hull Maritime Museum)

Early towage on the Humber waterways was by steam paddle tugs and the G&HSTC's *Shah* is shown in the 1900s ready to tow craft downriver to Hull. The vessel was built at South Shields in 1878 and originally had two funnels side by side. Hydraulic power was used to power the dock machinery and an accumulator tower lies to the left of this view.

The G&STC's steam tug *Goole No. 5* with a sea-going lighter in tow leaving Goole. Prior to the Second World War, this tug towed two coal-laden lighters down to the Thames each week.

A busy scene in the Ouse outside Goole Docks in the 1940s as steam tug *Goole No. 4* drops off the craft it has brought upriver from Hull after turning them head to tide. The craft will lock up into the docks and several will join an A&CNC merchandise tow to reach the Leeds or Wakefield wharves. (Humberside Libraries)

The G&HSTC's *Goole No.4* hauling an out-of-shot vessel from Ocean Lock into Goole Docks in the 1940s. After the Second World War, this tug was one of those used to tow Harkers' petrol tankers from Saltend to Leeds. (Humberside Libraries)

A 1950s scene in the Ouse off Goole as the motor vessel *Wesley* turns *Rosemary T.* and another Sheffield size keel head to tide prior to locking up into the docks and going via the A&CN, the New Junction Canal and S&SYN to Rotherham.

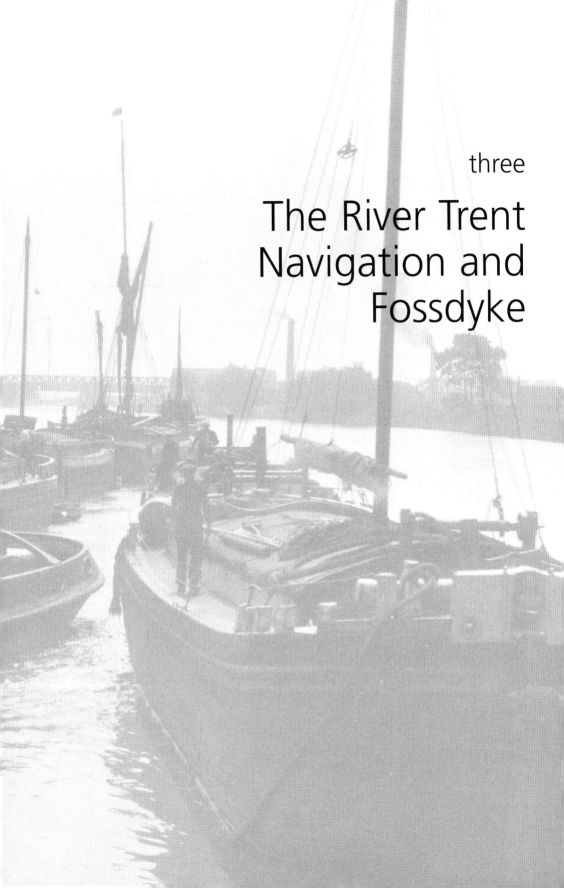

three

The River Trent Navigation and Fossdyke

At the dawn of the twentieth century, steam screw tugs owned by T. Gray & Co. provided a daily towing service from Hull through Gainsborough and further up the Trent to Torksey. Trent Navigation Co., owners of the navigation above Gainsborough, had their steam paddle tug *Robin Hood* take over craft bound further up the Trent at Torksey and pull them to the foot of Newark 'dyke', from where they were then poled or horse-hauled through Newark Nether Lock, up the dyke and through Town Lock to the TNC's transhipment depot where cargoes were transferred to shallow-draughted Upper Trent craft. After 1902, TNC's Clyde-built steam tug *Little John* then towed craft from there up to Nottingham. Grays' *Dalesman* was also hired to work above Newark for a time and, with the scrapping of *Robin Hood* in 1913, began covering the entire Torksey-Nottingham length.

Completion of four large locks between Newark and Nottingham in 1926 led to a demand for more extensive towing over this stretch; the establishment of new carrying companies, the building of new craft and the construction of a large water-served petroleum terminal at Colwick, below Nottingham. T. Gray & Co. became part of UTC in 1920 and they had new tugs built for work on the Trent. TNC constructed Trent Lane wharf and warehouse in Nottingham and made a marked policy change away from tugs with the building of three towing barges by Watsons of Gainsborough in the late 1920s.

In the 1930s and 1940s, TNC had further towing barges built. The final towage by pull-tug was done after the Second World War, when UTC satisfied Colwick's increasing demands by towing Harkers' dumb tankers from Saltend.

The building of a new lock at Newark with dimensions similar to those constructed earlier between the town and Nottingham removed a bottleneck which had prevented any vessel longer than 82½ft from passing above the town. Harkers then built bigger tankers to serve Colwick.

During the twentieth century, enormous tonnages of aggregate from both the Trent bed and numerous Trentside quarries were carried downriver by barge, mainly to wharves on the river Hull, but also on to the A&CN, especially in the 1980s and 1990s. Initially, craft used tugs, sails, the tide or a combination of two or all three of these to reach the quarries and return after loading. Lincoln & Hull Water Transport, however, built up a fleet of First World War steel-built, 200-ton capacity steam packets and used them to both carry cargoes and tow their dumb craft. After the Second World War, they bought more First World War craft in the shape of dumb, steel-built 'AC' (Ammunition Carrying) barges which, at first, were towed by the steam packets but were later motorised themselves to become towing barges before being phased out in the 1960s as a fleet of new self-propelled vessels was being introduced.

For the first half of the twentieth century, however, the greatest users of towage on the Trent were craft bound to or from Keadby. Some sea-going vessels also used the T. Gray/UTC public towing service to reach the Trent port and load coal from railway wagons, but, before nationalisation, large numbers of inland waterway craft, even some sailing craft, came from Hull behind a tug to reach the S&SYN via the entrance lock there and, eventually, return to Hull in similar fashion.

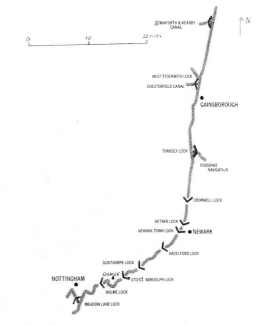

Right: A sketch map of the river Trent from Nottingham to near its confluence with the river Ouse to form the Humber.

Below: TNC's steam paddle tug *Robin Hood*, built on the river Thames in 1881, clearing barges grounded by low water levels at Collingham in 1912. A screw tug would have found it difficult to 'grip' in the shallow waters of the Trent hereabouts. (John Noble Collection)

RIVER TRENT NAVIGATION

TNC's *Little John*, designed for working in shallow waters with its twin propellers in small 'tunnels', towing 68ft x 14ft, shallow-draughted Upper Trent craft, which have raised their sails to assist the tug, at Fiskerton. These craft would have been loaded at Newark with cargoes brought from Hull by larger deeper-draughted craft and could work up to Burton-on-Trent or up the river Soar above Nottingham, to Loughborough and Leicester.

T. Gray & Co.'s steam tug *Bowman* approaching East and West Stockwith whilst coming down the Trent with a train of loaded barges in the 1900s.

One of T. Gray & Co.'s steam tugs hauling craft upriver through Gainsborough in the 1900s, bound for Torksey where vessels would either enter the Fossdyke to reach Lincoln or accept another tow to Newark.

UTC's *Ferryman*, built in Holland in 1914, purchased and renamed by UTC in 1926, hauling an upriver tow round Morton Corner, below Gainsborough, in the 1930s. Fortunately, Gainsborough's extensive coaster traffic that reached a peak between the 1960s and 1980s would not have been met by such a tow.

Opposite above: Watsons of Gainsborough built five dumb barges for Cammell Laird & Co. in 1927 to be used to transport 160 passenger coaches to Hull docks for export to India. UTC then began towing these over the whole Nottingham–Hull length of waterway using their twin-screw 2 x 78hp diesel tug *Motorman*, built by Henry Scarr of Hessle in 1925. *Motorman* is in attendance in 1927 as a coach is loaded onto one of the two barges moored by the riverside at Clifton, above Nottingham, prior to towing the pair to Hull.

Opposite below: UTC's *Motorman* towing a petrol tanker down the Trent below Gunthorpe in 1938, well after the railway coach work had ended. At this time, towage of petrol tankers comprised UTC's major Trent work. (John Noble Collection)

A general view of the river Trent outside the S&SYN entrance lock at Keadby in the 1930s with craft brought from Hull by UTC's steam tugs waiting to pen up into the canal as other vessels are being assembled for the tow back to Hull. A spritsail barge is waiting to load for the Thames near the coal chute on the riverbank to the left.

Built in 1915 and purchased by UTC in 1926, *Riverman* collects a tow of light craft off Keadby in the 1930s for its return voyage to Hull.

UTC's steam tug *Boatman*, built in 1923 by Cochranes of Selby, at Keadby in the 1930s. This tug helped *Motorman* on the Indian carriage contract. It turned over in 1935 on the Humber whilst helping to salvage the trawler *Edgar Wallace* and, after this, the steam engine was replaced by a 250hp diesel engine. This tug was one of the last to work on the Trent, towing petrol barges to Colwick until 1952. (John Noble Collection)

A UTC steam tug towing three craft down the Trent to Hull, approaches the point where Ouse and Trent join to form the Humber.

Charlie Johnson, boatman

In 1921, Dad's barge was usually loaded in Newark basin with cargoes from Hull brought by bigger boats. We were then towed up to Nottingham with other barges in a single line by *Little John* which went there and back six times a week. That tug drew only 2½ft. It had twin screws in tunnels and sometimes needed horses to help it in summer. I can remember the piles of coal it carried on deck, some of which was used to pelt cows standing in the river and shift them out of the navigation channel. The river got so low because locks above Newark at Hazleford, Gunthorpe, Stoke Bardolph and Holme had not been built then, though they had been staked out. Eventually things improved after soldiers who had recently returned from the war were employed constructing them.

Harry Day, tug broker

I began at Keadby in 1919 with an office on the jetty. Some craft occasionally sailed down to Hull but most used the tugs. Both tides were usually worked each day. I've known as many as fifty boats leaving here on a tide. Lincoln traders would have either sailed down from Torksey or driven down dragging their anchors and I'd have to get those on the canal out into the river to join them. You couldn't start until the flood came and, say it was high tide at six in the morning, I had to rouse the captains at three so they could be through the lock and ready, waiting for the tugs when they came up from Hull. On some days, three or four tugs would come up, each pulling eight keels in a V-formation. As soon as all those wanting to come onto the canal had got their lines ashore, one of the tugs would collect the boats that were for Gainsborough or Torksey and set off up the Trent with up to six of them in single file. The other tugs would hang their keels on and set off back to Hull. Part of my job was to check that every keel had two men aboard. Those who worked 'all-hands-one' on the canals had to hire a 'purchase man' for the Humber and some of them tried to dodge this. I was provided with a megaphone for shouting instructions to the skippers.

Joe Tomlinson, tug skipper

In the 1920s and '30s, keels loaded with coal for steam trawlers in the fish dock at Hull would be hung on to the end of one of the rows behind the tug when we left Keadby. As we got near Hull, the captains of these barges would judge when to let go. They needed just enough way on so that they could run alongside the dock jetty and get a rope ashore. They always seemed to judge this perfectly, though most of them had their anchors ready just in case. We dropped off other craft similarly at the other docks and Old Harbour entrance.

TNC's Trent size motor towing barge *Yare* on trials at Beckingham outside its builders' (Watsons of Gainsborough) yard in 1929. Sister craft *Stort* and *Tyne*, each designed to tow three craft, were built at the same time. TNC then had a fleet of three towing barges and twenty-nine dumb craft, boasted of a daily Hull–Nottingham service and ceased to use UTC for towage, leaving that company working on the Trent with only petrol tankers.

With ownership having passed first to the D&IWE on nationalisation and then to BTW, the towing barge *Tees* leaves Stoke Bardolph Lock whilst heading up the Trent to Nottingham in the 1950s. *Tees* was built for TNC in 1932 by Warrens of New Holland as a result of the success of the three earlier towing barges.

Direct Delivery Service was one of the first private companies formed to use the Trent up to Nottingham after construction of the new locks above Newark in the mid-1920s. Their Beverley-built, diesel-powered, iron towing barge *Direct* is shown in the Humber on acceptance trials in 1932.

Trent Carriers, another private Trent-based company, was formed in 1936, though their towing barge *Greendale*, shown here towing on the Humber in the 1950s, was built by Warrens of New Holland in 1932. (John Noble Collection)

Initially towing dumb craft purchased from Robert Teal of Carlton, Trent Carriers had dumb barges *William H. Gant*, *Nottingham Trader* and *Leicester Trader* built by Dunstons at Thorne in 1953. The former two are shown here coming up the Humber in the 1960s on a photograph taken from atop the mast of towing barge *Greendale*. (Jack Radford)

James W. Cook & Co.'s motor tanker barge *Curlew C.* photographed from the dumb tanker barge it was towing up the Trent to Colwick in 1938. (John Noble Collection)

The TNC had towing barges *Frank Rayner, Dee, Stour* and *Thames* built before nationalisation came in 1948. *Thames*, a 1947 product of D.E. Scarr of Howdendyke, is shown here off Hull. At 129ft x 17½ft, it was too long to pass through the Trent (size 82½ft x 14½ft) Newark Town Lock and up to Nottingham until a new lock was opened there in 1952. (John Noble Collection)

Opposite above: The 120ft x 16½ft steam packet *Omfleet*, Hessle-built for service during the First World War, was purchased in the 1920s by Lincoln & Hull Water Transport Co. The vessel, loaded with 200 tons of copper ore for Lincoln, is moored at Torksey where its cargo is to be transhipped into smaller craft for carriage along the Fossdyke. It will then travel further up the Trent to load aggregate from nearby quarries and tow a similarly loaded dumb vessel back to Hull. *Omfleet* was sunk by a mine in Alexandra Dock during the Second World War. (Alan Burman Collection)

Opppsite below: Lincoln & Hull's *Chas* (right) and *Kelfield* at Girton sand and gravel pit. The Liverpool-built steam packet *Chas* was another of the company's vessels designed for service in the First World War and had been converted to diesel power by the time this 1950s picture was taken. (John Noble Collection)

Now owned by the D&IWE, the former TNC's towing barge *Barlock*, built by Watsons in 1931 for Trent Concrete, with the three dumb vessels that it was towing, demonstrates the capacity of the new 190ft x 30ft Newark Town Lock, shortly after its opening in 1952. This removed a bottleneck by making it the same size as other locks on the navigation above Cromwell. (BWB)

Opposite above: The motor towing barge *Doris Clark* (see page 38) became Direct Delivery Service's *Delivery* in 1956 and is shown in the 1960s passing beneath Newark Town Bridge, bound for Nottingham. The vessel was owned by Acasters of Goole at the time. It was broken up in 1988. (Les Reid)

The towing barge *Maureen Eva* was built in 1962 by Hepworths of Paull, near Hull, for British Transport Waterways and is shown heading downriver on the Trent at Alston, above Newark in the 1960s with two craft in tow. The vessel was powered by a 150hp Gardner engine and worked for BWB until they ceased commercial carrying early in 1987, after which it was sold. (John Noble Collection)

Fossdyke

Torksey lock limited Lincoln-bound craft passing through it to reach the Fossdyke from the Trent to 74ft x 15½ft (Lincoln size).

For many years, the only towage on the Fossdyke was of small lighters into which cargo had been off-loaded, either above or below the lock at Torksey, to reduce a larger craft's draught and enable it to navigate to Lincoln. This was a common occurrence in the first half of the twentieth century when costs of labour for transhipment were minimal, at times when Trent water levels were high and the river could accommodate deeper-draughted vessels than the Fossdyke, perhaps because a ship had to be cleared of all its cargo to avoid delaying it at Hull. Initially towage of the lighters to Lincoln was then by either the larger craft or a small tug owned by Kendalls, the Lincoln boatbuilders and repairers.

After discharging at Lincoln and returning to Torksey, most craft would then be towed further up the Trent to collect a load of gravel for Hull before coming back downriver.

In the late 1920s, however, both Furley & Co. and Lincoln & Hull Water Transport Co., the two major carriers on the Fossdyke, purchased a small ex-naval vessel to act as a tug on the navigation in order to minimise delays to sailing craft when there was no fair wind. Furleys had *Eye* and Lincoln & Hull had *Cerebos*. These worked satisfactorily throughout the 1930s but had been phased out by the 1940s with the advent of powered craft.

Above: The Humber keel *Siddall*, owned by John Smith, sailing along the Fossdyke towards Lincoln with a small lighter in tow in the 1940s. Mast and sails would have to be lowered to pass beneath Saxilby Railway Bridge.

Right: A Lincoln size keel towing both lighter and cog boat along the Fossdyke towards Torksey in 1941.

Opposite below: Kendalls' small tug crossing Lincoln's Brayford in the 1910s.

Furley & Co.'s steam tug *Eye*, built in India, handling a dumb vessel in icy conditions on Lincoln's Brayford in the 1930s.

Opposite above: Eye on the Fossdyke in the late 1930s after a new wheelbox had been fitted by Scarrs of Hessle.

Opposite below: Lincoln & Hull Water Transport Co.'s steam tug *Cerebos* on the Fossdyke in the 1930s. Both this tug and *Eye* were notorious for causing long delays at Saxilby Swing Road Bridge as they pulled a long tow past at less than 1mph. (Alan Burman)

Lincoln & Hull's *Brayford*, seen making its way through the ice near Lincoln's Co-operative mill, below High Bridge, in the 1950s, occasionally towed dumb craft for the company after it had been motorised in 1948.

BWB's small diesel tug *Friar Tuck*, built at Wivenhoe in 1952 and normally based on the river Trent, on ice-breaking duties in 1954 as it tows a motor barge past a vessel moored at Lincoln BWB depot and into Brayford. (*Lincolnshire Echo*)

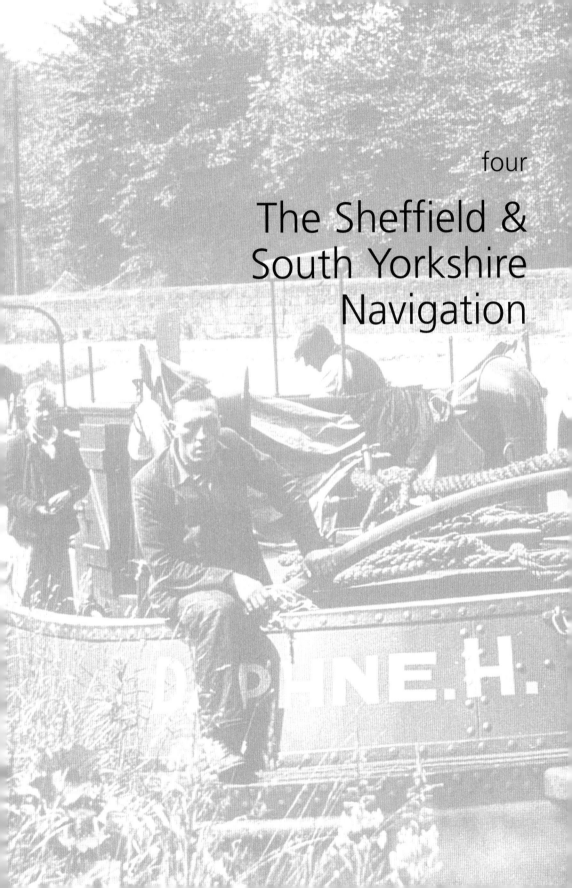

four

The Sheffield &
South Yorkshire
Navigation

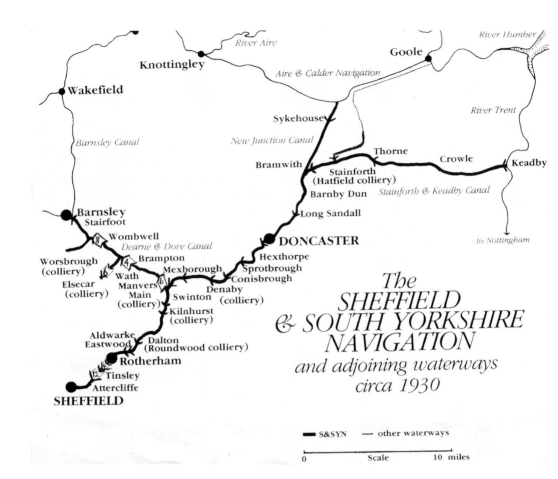

The
SHEFFIELD
& SOUTH YORKSHIRE
NAVIGATION
and adjoining waterways
circa 1930

■■ S&SYN — other waterways

0   Scale   10 miles

Much less towage took place on the S&SYN than on the A&CN, probably because all tows had to be passed through the S&SYN's 61½ft x 15½ft (Sheffield size) locks in single units, whereas, over the years, the A&CNC had lengthened their locks to accommodate tows unbroken.

Nevertheless, some steam towage by the Goole and Sheffield Transport Co.'s two tugs was undertaken before the First World War. Craft arriving at Keadby behind tugs owned by T. Gray & Co. and later, UTC (see page 52) were hauled to Doncaster and back via the Sheffield-size but well-separated locks at Thorne, Bramwith and Long Sandall. The majority of craft using the S&SYN joined it at Keadby but vessels from Goole were brought up the Dutch River and onto the S&SYN at Stainforth, below Bramwith Lock, before the 1905 opening of the New Junction Canal with its single 215ft-long lock. The lock at Stainforth between the S&SYN and Dutch River was closed due to lack of use in 1939, severing that link with Goole.

On rare occasions, UTC tugs ventured up the navigation in the 1920s and, throughout the 1930s, Trevethick's two diesel tugs which had come to the S&SYN after finishing work on the new Trent locks, provided a towing service between Keadby and Doncaster.

The A&CN's steam compartment tugs began working to Hatfield Colliery staithe in 1932 after Bramwith Lock had been lengthened to 215ft. But it was not until the 1950s that the compartment tugs brought the Tom Puddings to load at Doncaster in significant numbers after Long Sandall lock had been lengthened to 215ft in 1959.

The Goole & Sheffield Transport Co.'s steam tug *Don* working a tow of craft down Thorne Lock in the 1910s. *Clara Marion*, built in 1911 by Warrens of New Holland, succeeded *Don* on this towing service.

One of UTC's steam tugs, possibly *Norman* or *Irishman*, moored along with a keel and sloop at the limestone quarrying village of Levitt Hagg above Sprotbrough on the S&SYN in the 1920s. (Hugh Parkin Collection)

The 1894-built steam barge *Swift* was purchased by Edwin Bisby and worked as the Thorne market boat from the early 1920s until Boothferry Bridge was opened in 1929. Then it towed its owner's dumb craft to Gainsborough, Hull, Lincoln and Doncaster for over a decade and is shown ready to leave Keadby for Hull with *Harvester* and *Success* in tow. The vessel was subsequently converted to diesel power after purchase by Flixborough Shipping.

Built at Hessle by Scarrs in 1904 for the millers Rishworth, Ingleby and Lofthouse, the Sheffield size steam towing barge *Swiftsure* carried flour and towed similarly laden dumb barges from Hull to Rotherham. It is shown here, after being sold, moored at Thorne in the 1930s loaded with coal for Reckitts of Hull. Later still, it was purchased by the Hull coal merchants Rafferty & Watson and a diesel engine was installed in 1942.

Above: Harkers' Sheffield size, 70-ton capacity towing barge *Daphne H.*, especially built at Knottingley in 1936 for work on the S&SYN, prepares to leave Sprotbrough in 1938 with an out-of-shot dumb tanker bound for Sheffield. Both craft would be loaded with petrol for National Benzole's depot.

Right: In the late 1930s, when the motor/dumb tanker barge pair reached the foot of Tinsley's twelve-lock flight, the towing barge would go on ahead up to the 'top level' and along to the petrol depot, leaving the dumb vessel to follow, hauled by the S&SYNC's Tinsley-based tractor that had been introduced to speed up passage of craft through the flight. The vehicle, shown here in a manufacturer's brochure photograph, was built by Marshalls of Gainsborough and supplied with a winch and 50 yards of cable.

Above: G.D. Holmes's steam barge *Reliance* both carrying and towing barges loaded with Ouse-dredged sand up the New Junction Canal, bound for Pilkingtons, the glassmakers, at Long Sandall, near Doncaster in 1936.

Trevethick's other diesel tug *Tuna*, fitted with a 27hp Petter engine, running free through Stainforth in 1937. The tug occasionally towed up to Mexborough in flood conditions when river Don towpaths above Doncaster were underwater. It also hauled the S&SYN's dredging pans, and assisted at Dunstons' launches from Thorne boatyard.

Opposite below: W. Trevethick's 1902-built 90hp diesel tug *Sulzer* was based at Keadby in the 1930s and offered a public towing service to Doncaster. Its captain, Herbert Moxon, and his wife-to-be are shown aboard the vessel as it heads up the Stainforth & Keadby section of the S&SYN towards Thorne. The tug was bought by Harkers and used throughout the Second World War to tow their dumb petrol tankers.

The lengthening of the S&SYN's Bramwith Lock in 1932, led to coal from Hatfield Colliery becoming readily accessible by the puddings and here, in 1935, a steam compartment tug is hauling a train of loaded pans towards the lock, bound for Goole via the New Junction Canal. (BWB)

Opposite above: Hanleys, the Doncaster millers, decided to add a 100hp diesel towing barge to their fleet of sailing craft and Dunstons built *Hanleys Pride* for them in 1937. The vessel is shown in the Trent at Keadby, with towropes taut whilst en route from Hull to Doncaster.

Opposite below: After waterborne deliveries of coal on the L&LC to Kirkstall Power Station (see page 24) diminished, some of their 'white boats' were brought to the S&SYN in the mid-1950s to deliver coal from a lorry-fed staithe at Mexborough to the newly opened power station at Campsall Fields, Doncaster. The towing barge *No.23* and a dumb barge are shown leaving Sprotbrough Lock on this traffic.

Above: Waddingtons of Swinton eventually took over coal supplies to Doncaster power station and their motor barge *Heritage* tows dumb barge *No. 8* away from Sprotbrough Lock in 1978. A total of over 200 tons of coal is being carried and Victor Waddington always maintained that usage of pairs of motor/dumb craft with one small engine between them was the most efficient way of working at this time through the Sheffield-size S&SYN locks above Doncaster.

Right: Teal, one of BWB's small diesel tugs, helping with pans at Doncaster's lorry-fed compartment boat staithe. The crane barge visible is grabbing out smokeless fuel from a pan sunk when a careless lorry driver tipped too much of his load into it.

Below: BWB's diesel-engined compartment tug *Kellingley* approaching Long Sandall lock, lengthened in 1959, with a train of loaded Tom puddings bound for Goole in 1977.

Opposite below: Robert P. Rishworth, built for Spillers by Scarrs of Howdendyke in 1956 and lengthened in 1966, with dumb barge R37 fastened alongside, passes through West Dock, Goole, in 1987. Both vessels, having passed to Holgates, are loaded with steel from Rotherham for export. After the S&SYN Improvement Scheme of the 1980s the two craft could pass through new locks on the navigation without breaking the tow.

BWB's diesel compartment tug *Wheldale* towing a train of barges up an ice-choked New Junction Canal in early 1963.

One of the diesel compartment tugs approaching Sykehouse lift bridge as it brings loaded pans down an icy New Junction Canal bound for Goole from Doncaster in 1981.

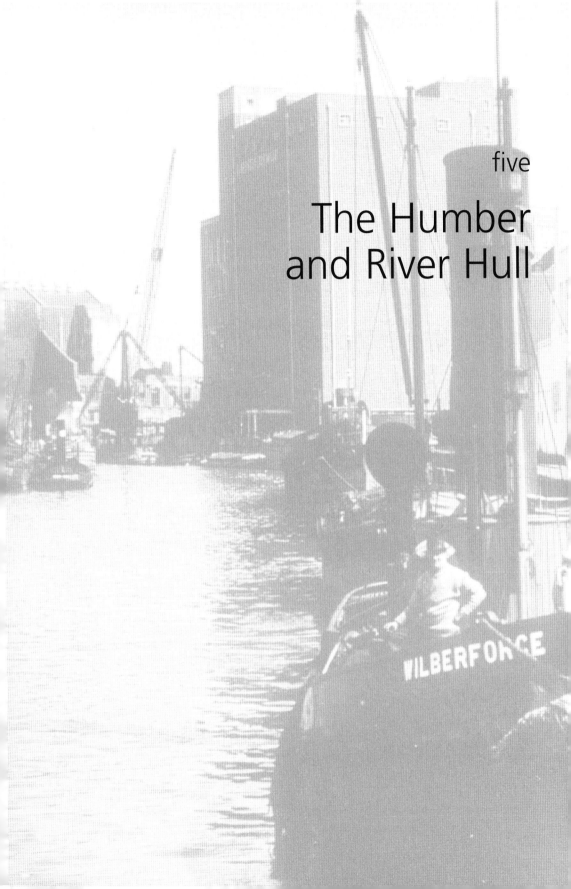

five

The Humber
and River Hull

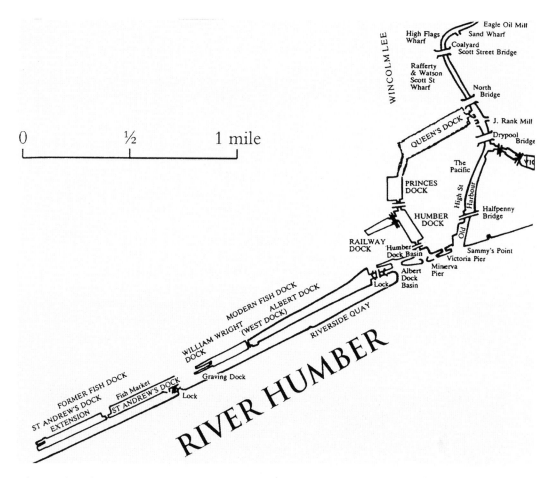

Above: A plan of Hull's western docks, piers and Old Harbour (the lower reaches of the river Hull before it enters the Humber).

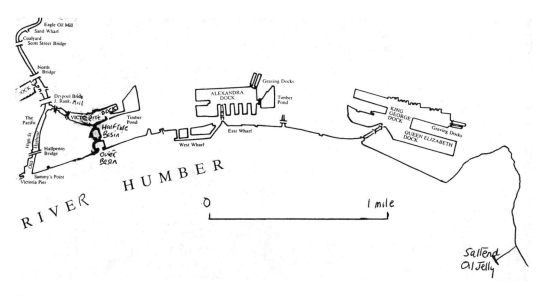

Hull was a centre of tug activity on the Humber waterways during the early years of the twentieth century. Discounting the docking tugs which handled shipping, there were river tugs working up to the Trent and Ouse and the local harbour tugs. The latter, owned by companies such as John Deheer and Foster Tow, handled barges and lighters on the lower reaches of the river Hull and delivered them to and from the various docks as required. This third type of towage, which served the numerous industrial premises lining the lower couple of miles of the river, lasted well into the 1970s, by which time the other two types had considerably diminished in their extent.

There was a permanent display on the river Hull of the great advantage of leaving a relatively cheap loaded vessel tied up at a wharf to be discharged whilst the much more expensive powered unit was not similarly out of action but able to continue working with other craft.

As on other waterways, diesel tugs began taking over from steam tugs in the 1920s and towing barges followed a similar trend, becoming even more popular than tugs.

Peter Foster's tugs were taken over by UTC in 1954 and, in 1964, Gilyott & Scott became established as major tug and lighter owners by amalgamation of the companies of William Gilyott, John A. Scott, T.F. Wood, Furleys and John Deheer. Lighterage on the river Hull virtually ended in the 1980s due to a number of factors, including implementation of the Devlin Report, industrial unrest and the abolition of free overside loading to inland waterway craft in the docks.

Above: Some idea of the variety of towing at Hull in the early 1930s may be gathered from this aerial view of the Humber looking across Minerva and Corporation piers into the Old Harbour.

Opposite below: A plan of Hull's eastern docks, also showing Saltend oil jetty.

John A. Scott's 60ft x 14ft, 1895-built steam tug *Edith*, hauling lighters loaded from sea-going vessels in Hull's Albert Dock through the entrance lock and into the Humber for delivery to Old Harbour premises. At this time, Scotts' had several large warehouses as well as the largest fleet of lighters on the river Hull and *Edith*, their sole tug, was also the usual handler of lighters owned by the LNER, Ranks and the Co-op.

Right: The 30ft-long diesel tug *Fear Not*, a wooden ex-fishing drifter owned by James Barraclough, lies moored in the Old Harbour. The vessel towed Ranks' lighters across the Humber to the river Ancholme and thence to Brigg and also worked up the Trent to Gainsborough and the S&SYN as far as Mexborough, before being sold to Harkers in 1939 to handle their Leeds-bound dumb tankers during the Second World War.

Below: John Deheer's 1930s billhead lists his steam tugs. As well as handling lighters owned by the Premier Oil Extraction Mills, BOCM and RIL (later Spillers), this company also performed Scotts' surplus work with other companies' lighters.

CONTRACTORS TO THE AIR MINISTRY AND ON THE ADMIRALTY LISTS.

18 HIGH STREET,
HULL, *April* 11 1940.

TELEGRAMS: "SALVOR, HULL."

TELEPHONES:
OFFICE · · · − 15614
MANAGER'S RESIDENCE − − 36552
ALEXANDRA DOCK − − 31021
TUG BROKER · · · − 32418

Messrs Waddington

Dr. to JOHN DEHEER LIMITED

OWNERS OF THE SCREW STEAM TUGS

For Towing as over. "FAIRY," "IAN," "MUSCOVITE" & "ROVER"

FITTED WITH SALVAGE PUMPS.

Date	Name or No. of Vessel	From	To	Rate	£	s.	d.
April 11	*Serenity*	*Hail*	*Alex*			10	3
		Received. — *PP J Deheer Ltd*					
		S · Boothly					

A UTC steam tug moored in the 1920s at low water near the entrance to the Old Harbour. The picture also shows South (or Halfpenny) Bridge, the lowest road crossing of the river Hull, which was opened in 1865, closed in 1934 and demolished ten years later.

Two paddle tugs are seen in the Old Harbour looking downriver from Drypool Bridge in the 1890s. *Heather Bell* was built on the Tyne at North Shields in 1857, bought from Aberdeen owners by William Elliot, and moved to Hull in 1889. The twin-funnelled *True Briton* was built on the Thames in 1854, bought from London owners by T. Gray, and repositioned at Hull in 1876. By 1897, both craft had been scrapped.

Looking down the Old Harbour in the 1920s towards South Bridge from a similar viewpoint to the previous picture. There are fewer warehouses evident, tugs and lighters are moored at High Street wharves and, at the left, a steam towing barge is loading at Ranks' Clarence Mills whilst another waits astern of it.

RIL's steam towing barge *John M. (Rishworth)* lies almost ready for launching at Scarrs' Hessle Yard in 1915. The 92ft x 15½ft vessel was steered from amidships. Other steel towing barges built at Hessle for the company were *Eagle*, *Swan* and *Cygnet*. All carried flour from their owners' Swan mills in the Old Harbour to Grimsby, Leeds, Wakefield and York. By 1928, RIL and these craft had become part of Spillers.

Above: Three steam tugs are partly visible, as well as two of Harkers' tankers, on this 1930s photograph taken from Hull's High Street wharves. The tugs are Fosters' *Acetut*, built in 1886 for the Hull & Barnsley Railway Co., Whitakers' 1885-built *Cawood*, acquired by them from the Humber Pilotage Service in 1912, and Deheers' *Ian*, formerly Grays' *Irishman*, built in 1900. (Whitakers)

Right: In 1948, Whitakers purchased a 78ft x 15½ft coal-fired 240hp steam tug from the Admiralty and named it *Ackworth*. The vessel did similar work to *Wilberforce* and is shown in the 1950s moored at the Old Harbour's High Street wharves. (Whitakers)

Opposite above: John H. Whitaker's Yorkshire Dry Dock subsidiary built the 65ft x 15ft coal-fired steam tug *Wilberforce* in 1920 at their yard in the Old Harbour. The tug towed its owner's and the oil mills' dry cargo lighters between Hull and Selby and also bunkered ships by taking oil lighters into Hull docks, providing steam to work their pumps. Here, it is moored near the mouth of the river Hull in the early 1950s. The tug was converted to oil-firing in 1953 and scrapped in 1961. (Albert Richards Collection)

Whitakers had a 200hp diesel engine installed in *Cawood* during 1953 and the tug is shown in the Humber on its subsequent trials. (Whitakers)

Henry Dawson, harbour tug Edith at work in the late 1930s

The tug would be moored between tides at the mouth of the Old Harbour and an hour or so before the tide began to flow, one of the crew would come aboard and see to the fire. He would be joined by the rest of the four-man crew as soon as the vessel began to float and they'd set off down the Humber, perhaps with a couple of lighters in tow, to Alex or King George Dock. After dropping off the lighters, the tug would wait outside the dock entrance lock.

At busy times, only river traffic heading for the Trent and Ouse would be in the first locking down at four hours before high water and the tug's crew could only watch as the United Towing Co. and Goole tugs collected craft that their brokers had booked them to tow upriver. These then moved off to another dock entrance lock to collect more craft and marshal their tows into two lines, in an arrangement that the brokers had previously instructed the barge captains to adopt, before setting off up the Humber. Sometimes, the Trent tugs would have to round up between Victoria Dock and the harbour mouth to collect a Thames spritty barge that was riding at anchor waiting for a tow up to Keadby to load coal.

By this time, the lock would have been turned round and more river craft wanting to leave the dock would have locked down to Humber level. *Edith* would then be able to back into the lock after this second penning and collect its craft which would then be towed upriver in one line, with vessels 10ft or so apart. If any craft had to be collected from the Town docks or Albert Dock, the tow would be tied up outside Victoria Dock while the tug went to collect them and bring them back to join the tow.

On big tides, the tug would then tow upriver past the harbour mouth to Victoria pier before turning head to tide to bring its tow into and up the Old Harbour as far as Victoria Dock basin or between Drypool and North Bridges. Here the lighters would be 'knocked off'. Each one would turn head-to-tide and move stern-first upriver to its berth, using the tide and a mud weight trailing from its bows to give steerage and control speed.

The tug would then go 2 miles up the river Hull to Stoneferry and collect empty lighters from various wharves as it came back downriver over the tide. Some of these would then be moored outside Scotts' warehouse below Drypool Bridge, if not required in the docks, or taken to the docks. *Edith* would perhaps return to the Old Harbour with loaded lighters that had not finished loading in time for the earlier pennings out of the dock and had come out into the Humber after the tide had ceased to flow and water in the dock and river had made a level.

After coaling from its owners' coal hulk, the tug would then return to its between-tides mooring at the harbour mouth and tie up as the water ebbed away before eventually sitting on the mud.

A steam tug towing empty lighters out of the Old Harbour, bound for Hull's eastern docks. The New Holland paddle steamer ferry lies at Victoria Pier. (*Hull Daily Mail*)

A UTC steam tug towing a sailing barge from the entrance lock to its berth in Hull's King George Dock about a decade after its 1914 opening. River and harbour tugs rarely entered the docks, preferring to drop off in-going craft in the river and pick them up there again when they had penned back out after their visits. Movement of these craft about the dock was performed manually using poles and ropes. Any rare 'snatches' they could beg from moving powered vessels were most welcome.

Grimsby's docks were never as busy with inland waterway craft as those at Hull, though RIL's steam keels towed lighters across the Humber from Hull and Whitakers' tugs and lighters did much business bunkering fishing vessels there. 'Blow's Hull & Grimsby Steamers', however, were based in the town and their lighters and steam towing barges *Basalt* and *Quenast* provided a cross-Humber cargo service. The former vessel is shown at the company's Grimsby Riverhead landing in the 1930s discharging a cargo for onward delivery by horse and dray.

Blows' steamer *Quenast* at Grimsby's Riverhead in the 1940s with one of their lighters partly visible to the right. Bagged flour was carried from Hull to Spillers' mill at Grimsby and seeds for crushing, imported via Hull's docks, were delivered to Sowerby's oil mill. A similar towing barge/lighter service was also provided by the Grimsby Express Packet Co., using the steamers *Trent* and *WN*.

A lighter has successfully negotiated a 'snatch' from the captain of the former TNC motor barge *Yare* after loading in Hull's King George Dock during the 1960s. (*Hull Daily Mail*)

Gilyott & Scott's motorised lighter *Kelena* built in 1923 by Warrens of New Holland and motorised in 1962, brings two of the company's lighters into the King George & Queen Elizabeth Dock entrance lock in 1981, bound up the Humber for the Old Harbour.

The towing barge *Frederick Oldridge*, built by Hepworths of Paull in 1956 for William Gilyott & Co., is shown towing a couple of lighters up the Old Harbour below Drypool Bridge in 1979.

The diesel tug *Gillian Knight* was built in 1963 by the Drypool Engineering & Dry Dock Co. for Scotts. After passing beneath Drypool Bridge, the tug has cast off its upriver tow and is preparing to head back downriver as the lighters it has brought prepare to turn head-to-tide and begin driving beneath North Bridge to reach their destinations further up the river Hull.

Now owned by Gilyott & Scott, the tug *Gillian Knight* hauls the lighter *Tit* beneath Drypool Bridge in 1979, en route for King George Dock. Lighters often had the advantage, shown here, of being able to slip beneath the Old Harbour's lift bridges at early stages of a tide without disrupting road traffic by requiring them to be raised.

The former grain barge *John M. (Rishworth)* (see page 91) had its wheelhouse re-sited and original steam engine replaced by a diesel unit before the Second World War. It is shown on the Humber in 1979 with the dumb *Leethams' Pat*, another former grain barge, fastened alongside. Both craft were owned by Holgates at the time.

Holgates' *John M.* and *Florence* on Aldwarke weir on the river Don, near Rotherham in late 1989 after breaking loose from their moorings on the S&SYN and drifting downriver. A huge crane was brought from 50 miles away at 1mph to lift the vessels back onto the navigation.

The historic, 1906-built tug *Primrose* at work in Hull's Albert Dock in 1992. Originally a coal-fired steam tug, the vessel spent most of its working life based at Sharpness on the river Severn. A 350hp diesel engine was fitted in 1960, but the vessel was laid up in 1979. Subsequently, it came to the Humber area and worked mainly at Selby. Then it was purchased to tow a coal barge between Glasson Dock, near Lancaster and the Isle of Man, returning to the Humber after acquisition by John Dean in 1991.

six

Early
Push Tugs

Several of the ninety-one innovative Bantam tugs built between 1951 and 1969 by
E.C. Jones & Son came to the Humber waterways region, to handle workboats on various
BWB navigations and aggregate barges in quarries. Bantams ranged in size from 16ft x 7ft to
38ft x 13½ft.

Cawoods Hargreaves had the UK's first large push-towed fleet built between 1964 and 1968,
when Richard Dunston of Thorne produced thirty-five 170-ton capacity dumb barges and nine
rectangular plan 29ft x 14ft push tugs fitted with 150hp Dorman diesel engines driving a fully
rotating propeller unit which also steered the vessel. The system brought coal to Ferrybridge
C Power Station and was a development of the A&CNC's compartment boat operation with
a single hoist able to lift the pans bodily to discharge cargoes. Well over a million tons were
brought each year in three-pan units from nearby loading staithes by a service which began in
1967 and ended in 2002.

Loaded trains were pushed by the tugs, light trains were usually pulled, giving the helmsman
better visibility by avoiding him having to look over pans riding high in the water. Tonnages were
affected by miners' strikes in 1974 and 1984 and the hoist was out of action for most of 1973
when one empty pan was lowered onto another that had been blown back under it. Nevertheless,
a total of over 43 million tons were delivered during the whole period of operation.

The BTC's Bantam tug *Eric of Lincoln* is launched into the Trent in 1958
from the lorry that had delivered it from its Brentford builders. (E.C. Jones
& Son)

BWB's Bantam tug *Alan-a-Dale*, built in 1957, pushing a dredgings pan past High Marnham Power Station on the river Trent in 1983.

Bantam tug, the 1953-built *No.28*, pushing an aggregate-filled dumb barge away from the loading staithe on the river Soar navigation at Thurmaston, near Leicester, in 1994. Each day, 600 tons were carried over a mile downriver to a screening plant with three Bantam tugs involved.

Old and new compartment boats are photographed side by side on the A&CN's Castleford Cut, above Bulholme lock in 1968. Push tug *CH 105* and three loaded Cawoods Hargreaves' compartment boats, are carrying a total of about 510 tons of coal and the Tom Pudding train hauled by a diesel tug, is holding 600–700 tons. (Norman Burnitt)

In the late 1960s, experiments were made with four-pan tows on the A&CN and here, *CH 109* approaches Knostrop Fall lock from below with such an assembly. (Norman Burnitt)

Cawoods Hargreaves push tug *CH 102* holds a pan beneath the loading chute in Fryston Colliery basin in 1985, shortly before the colliery there closed. The tugs' original Dorman engines had been replaced with 160hp Kelvins by this time.

CH 103 and three Kellingley-loaded pans head beneath the old Great North Road Bridge at Ferrybridge, bound for the C Station hoist, in 1980.

For an eleven-month period in 1993–94, Cawoods Hargreaves' craft used the S&SYN to load at Eastwood, near Rotherham. *CH 107* is shown in November 1993 with a loaded train negotiating the right-angled bend at Double Bridges, Mexborough, en route for Ferrybridge.

CH 104, acting as the hoist shunt tug at Ferrybridge, helping to turn the tow that *CH 103* has brought upriver from Kellingley Colliery prior to it being placed in the channel for tipping in 1986.

A view of the channel beneath the tipping hoist at Ferrybridge C Power Station, taken in 1996 from the tug that has brought the three-pan train from Kellingley Colliery. A train of three pans could be discharged in thirty minutes.

BWB Push Tows, including BACAT

Impressed by Cawoods Hargreaves' adoption of push towing, BWB used a couple of their towing barges to experiment with the procedure. As a result, they built two tugs at their Goole yard 'to overcome problems of delays to craft'. In their 1969 Annual Report, it was then indicated that they proposed to convert their entire General Merchandise Fleet to this system.

The tugs, unlike the Bantams and those of Cawoods Hargreaves, each had two 150hp engines. These were linked to rotating Schottel steering units fitted in positions that made them very vulnerable to damage in shallow water.

After several years of planning, the BACAT (Barge Aboard CATamaran) and LASH (Lighter Aboard SHip) systems were introduced onto the Humber with a mother ship carrying the inland waterway craft across the North Sea to and from Rotterdam. The UK operation was based at Hull's Riverside Quay with BACAT and LASH craft pushed to their destinations at ports such as Doncaster, Nottingham, Gainsborough and Selby by the two Goole-built tugs and two 420hp tugs purchased from the Port of London Authority. Two ex-compartment boat tugs which had become surplus to requirements as coal, formerly shipped from Goole to the Thames, was being replaced by North Sea gas, were fitted with pusher 'knees' and used to help with BACAT barges on the A&CN and S&SYN.

Unfortunately, Hull dockers took great exception to this early form of containerisation and blacked the system, killing it off within eighteen months of its 1974 start. The tugs involved then reverted to general canal work.

BWB's two Goole-built push tugs *Freight Pioneer* and *Freight Trader* on the S&SYN above Aldwarke lock. *Trader*, with towrope passing through the lock gates, illustrates the laborious method of working a train unit-by-unit through the Sheffield size lock. As well as handling BACAT barges on the S&SYN, these two tugs also worked them on the A&CN to Leeds and, occasionally, up the Trent to Nottingham.

Opposite below: BWB's Goole-built tug *Freight Pioneer*, launched in 1970, heads towards the (then) swing bridge at Barnby Dun, below Doncaster, in the early 1970s, bound for Rotherham with three loaded BACAT-type dumb barges.

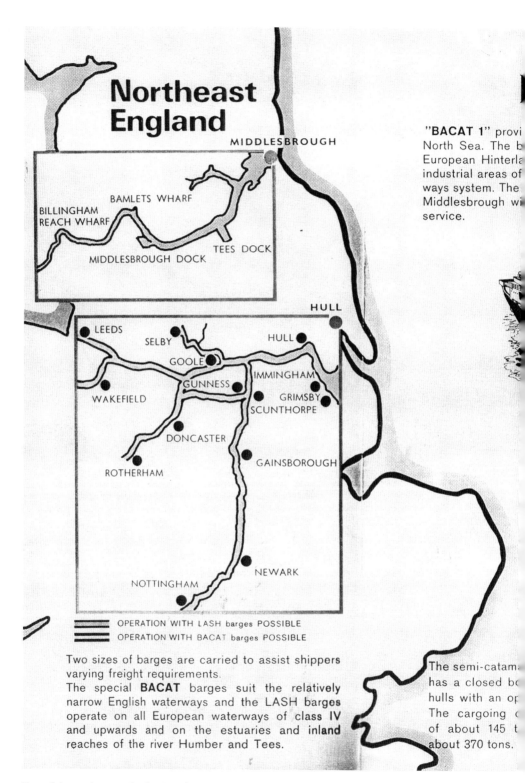

Northeast England

MIDDLESBROUGH

BAMLETS WHARF

BILLINGHAM
REACH WHARF

TEES DOCK

MIDDLESBROUGH DOCK

HULL

LEEDS

SELBY

GOOLE

HULL

IMMINGHAM

GUNNESS

WAKEFIELD

GRIMSBY

SCUNTHORPE

DONCASTER

GAINSBOROUGH

ROTHERHAM

NEWARK

NOTTINGHAM

OPERATION WITH LASH barges POSSIBLE
OPERATION WITH BACAT barges POSSIBLE

"BACAT 1" provi
North Sea. The b
European Hinterl∈
industrial areas of
ways system. The
Middlesbrough wi
service.

Two sizes of barges are carried to assist shippers
varying freight requirements.
The special **BACAT** barges suit the relatively
narrow English waterways and the LASH barges
operate on all European waterways of class IV
and upwards and on the estuaries and inland
reaches of the river Humber and Tees.

The semi-catam:
has a closed b⁢
hulls with an o⁣
The cargoing c
of about 145 t
about 370 tons.

Part of the explanatory leaflet issued to publicise the BACAT system.

CAT LINE

...r service across the
...arries link Northern
...lands and Northern
...ng the inland water-
...Hull, Rotterdam and
...e gateways for the

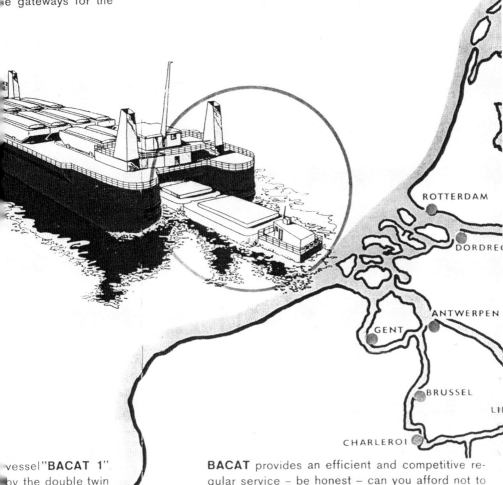

ROTTERDAM

DORDRE(

ANTWERPEN

GENT

BRUSSEL

LI(

CHARLEROI

...vessel "BACAT 1".
...by the double twin

...0 BACAT barges
...ASH barges of

BACAT provides an efficient and competitive regular service – be honest – can you afford not to use **BACAT?**
For additional information, freight rates and conditions, please contact the **BACAT** agents listed on the back of this brochure.

The System

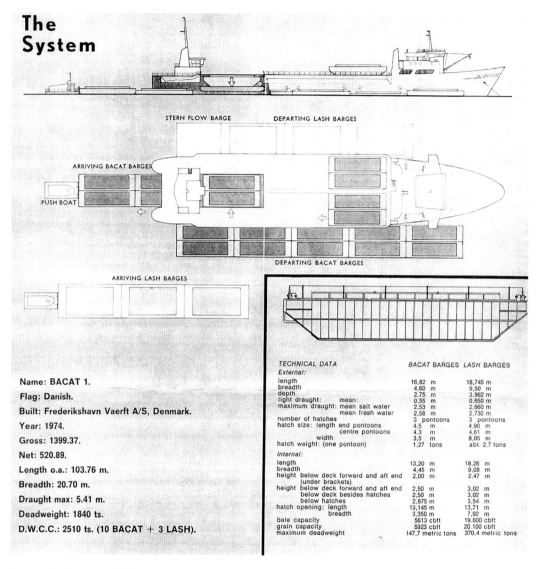

STERN FLOW BARGE   DEPARTING LASH BARGES

ARRIVING BACAT BARGES

PUSH BOAT

DEPARTING BACAT BARGES

ARRIVING LASH BARGES

Name: **BACAT 1.**

Flag: **Danish.**

Built: **Frederikshavn Vaerft A/S, Denmark.**

Year: **1974.**

Gross: **1399.37.**

Net: **520.89.**

Length o.a.: **103.76 m.**

Breadth: **20.70 m.**

Draught max: **5.41 m.**

Deadweight: **1840 ts.**

D.W.C.C.: **2510 ts. (10 BACAT + 3 LASH).**

TECHNICAL DATA		BACAT BARGES	LASH BARGES
External:			
length		16,82 m	18,745 m
breadth		4,60 m	9,50 m
depth		2,75 m	3,962 m
light draught:	mean:	0,55 m	0,650 m
maximum draught:	mean salt water	2,53 m	2,660 m
	mean fresh water	2,58 m	2,730 m
number of hatches		3 pontoons	3 pontoons
hatch size: length	end pontoons	4,5 m	4,90 m
	centre pontoons	4,3 m	4,61 m
	width	3,5 m	8,05 m
hatch weight: (one pontoon)		1,27 tons	abt. 2,7 tons
Internal:			
length		13,20 m	18,26 m
breadth		4,45 m	9,08 m
height below deck forward and aft end		2,00 m	2,47 m
(under brackets)			
height below deck forward and aft end		2,50 m	3,02 m
below deck besides hatches		2,50 m	3,02 m
below hatches		2,875 m	3,54 m
hatch opening: length		13,145 m	13,71 m
breadth		3,350 m	7,92 m
bale capacity		5613 cbft	19.600 cbft
grain capacity		5923 cbft	20.100 cbft
maximum deadweight		147,7 metric tons	370,4 metric tons

Further details of the BACAT system from the publicity leaflet.

Opposite above: BWB purchased the Port of London tugs *Placer* and *Plausible*, built in 1968 at Wivenhoe, to help with the BACAT operation. These retained their 420hp Rolls-Royce engines and Schottel units but were renamed *Freight Endeavour* and *Freight Mover* respectively. They needed too much headroom to pass beneath canal bridges and were usually kept on river work to Gainsborough and Selby. *Endeavour* is shown feeding BACAT barges into the mother ship in 1974.

Above: Three BWB push-tugs and the sea-going tug *Dunheron*, which BWB hired to help with the mother ship, performing a BACAT operation off Hull in the mid-1970s. The larger dumb craft visible are LASH barges.

Ken Tipton, BACAT tug skipper

The BACAT mother ship did five trips a fortnight across the North Sea and back, and, as we were pushing barges down to Hull, we'd often hear it over the radio requesting a pilot to bring it up the Humber again. A few hours later and we'd be off back up the river with loaded barges and no time for rest. To keep the ship serviced, we often had to move when there really wasn't enough water in the rivers. When a six-barge tow grounded on Whitton Sands, the ropes broke and two of the craft floated off up to Trent Falls. After that, four was made the maximum tow.

BACAT barges brought a lot of steel and furnace additives to Doncaster. Rotherham would have been closer to the Sheffield steelworks but the Improvement Scheme was a long way off and it was a day's extra work going up there from Doncaster, one barge at a time through those small locks, and another day extra coming back. Also, we could get 140-ton loads to Doncaster but only 100 tons to Rotherham. There was always a problem balancing imports and exports. The main exports from the S&SYN were wire coils, scrap steel, tractors built in Doncaster and tractor parts.

BACAT delivered structural steel and general cargo to Leeds and mica to Nottingham, and LASH carried Soya beans to Selby and fertiliser to Gainsborough but there was little exported from these places.

Hull dockers killed BACAT. We had to take two loaded barges and two empties into the docks on each visit by the ship, then they transferred the cargoes from the full barges to the empties. Eventually, they got sick of this, just lifted the lids and claimed they'd done it. Their demands became even dafter and customers were frightened off.

A diesel ex-compartment tug seen from Conisbrough railway viaduct on the S&SYN pushes three ex-BACAT dumb boats loaded with a 'pretend' cargo up the river Don in the early 1980s on a photograph used to publicise the improved navigation. (BWB)

Opposite: With the advent of North Sea gas, the compartment boats began moving away from coal in 1967 to smaller tonnages of smokeless fuel, leaving some tugs surplus to requirements. BWB's former diesel compartment tug, *West Riding*, with its 135hp Lister Blackstone engine and recently fitted pusher knees, both pulling and pushing Rotherham-bound craft above the Sheffield-size Aldwarke lock, having taken a total of fifty minutes for all four units to pen up.

After lying almost idle since the BACAT operation finished, two ex-BACAT tugs were employed on construction of the Humber Bridge. *Freight Pioneer* is shown, in early 1980, pushing a pontoon carrying a section of the bridge up the Humber. (*Hull Daily Mail*)

After working on construction of the Humber Bridge, *Freight Endeavour*'s retractable wheelbox was lowered and fixed in 1980 to allow the tug to pass beneath bridges on the A&CN and S&SYN. The tug is shown here below Bulholme lock pushing two barges loaded at Knostrop depot, near Leeds, towards Goole.

seven

Push Tows
after the 1970s

In the 1980s and 1990s, several established canal carriers decided to become involved with push-towing as they realised the economic advantages of shifting a cargo using one large dumb barge instead of a number of smaller self-propelled craft. The large S&SYN locks (254ft x 23ft), built as part of the Improvement Scheme in the early 1980s, also made that waterway able at last to accommodate push-tows unbroken.

In almost a reversal of their early 1960s policy to convert new 200-ton capacity dumb barges to motor barges, Hargreaves decided in the early 1980s to remove the engines from six of these and fit six others with more powerful engines, thus enabling these to push-tow the dumb vessels produced. The decision was prompted by an EU ruling on the manning of inland waterway craft.

Branford Barge Services and Waddingtons were amongst other operators who chose to have one of their motor barges push a dumb barge and both Acaster's Water Transport and Waddingtons separately converted a pull-tug and a cut-down motor barge into push tugs. Acasters even built a new push tug in 1996 for work mainly between Goole and York.

In 1998, John Dean reintroduced LASH barges onto the Humber with a feeder ship handling craft between an Atlantic-crossing mother ship at Rotterdam and Immingham. Amongst other tugs, purchased for the operation by 'Dean's Tugs', the sister tugs *Lashette* and *Shovette* came from the Medway owners who had handled LASH traffic on that Kent river until the service there was withdrawn.

Hargreaves motor barge *Susan* and dumb barge *No.6* loading Australian coal for Ferrybridge B Power Station at Wakefield in 1989. The coal had been brought to Wakefield by lorry from a ship at Keadby on the Trent that had transhipped it at Rotterdam. A tanker may also be seen discharging a cargo of oil.

Opposite above: Hargreaves' *Katharine* pushing *No.6* out of Savile Colliery basin in 1985. Both vessels are loaded with coal for Ferrybridge B Power Station.

Above: Hargreaves' *Susan*, embarrassingly low in the water, at the confluence of the rivers Aire and Calder, pushing the company's temporarily indisposed motor barge *Laura* into Castleford flood lock in 1983. Both craft are loaded with coal for Ferrybridge B Power Station. These push-towed pairs finished work in 1991 as Ferrybridge B Power Station closed.

John Branford's *Cordale*, loaded with building sand, pushes his dumb ex-lighter *Claire*, carrying silica sand, up the A&CN near New Bridge in late 1987, bound for Bank Dole wharf at Knottingley. The latter cargo was one of the last of many brought up the canal throughout most of the twentieth century by Branfords for glassworks at Knottingley. (Mike Brown)

The former pull-tug *Jumsey*, built in Holland during 1928 for Southampton owners, was purchased in the 1980s by Waterlink and fitted to push-tow ex-BACAT pans that the company had bought. It is seen here in 1990, on a picture taken from Knottingley's Mill Bridge, pushing the temporarily indisposed motor barge *Syenite*, loaded with Trent aggregate, up the A&CN towards Ferrybridge Power Stations, bound for Leeds. (Andy Horn)

Waddingtons' motor barge *Felix* pushing their engineless *Loxley* in 1980 near Doncaster Power Station, where their loads of Denaby coal will be discharged.

The tanker *Kingfisher C.* was cut down and converted to the push-tug *Kingfisher* at Waddingtons' Swinton yard, designed to push the barge *Confidence* carrying a 333-ton casting from Goole to Doncaster. The first of four of these is passing Rawcliffe Bridge on the A&CN in December 1982.

Leaving Long Sandall Lock, Waddingtons' former compartment tug *Allerton Bywater*, renamed *Strongbow*, pushes the dumb barge *Resilience*, loaded with 500 tons of imported fluorspar, from Goole to Rotherham in 1997.

Wadddingtons *Progress* (ex-Harkers' *Ennerdale H.*) pushing the company's dumb barge *Vivos* up the S&SYN, waits to pen up Sprotbrough Lock in 1999. Both vessels were loaded with fluorspar for Rotherham. Unlike the pre-1980s situation, craft longer than 61½ft could venture above Doncaster and, furthermore, there would have been no need to break this tow at any of the locks encountered on the voyage from Goole. BWB's Bantam tug *Eric of Lincoln,* pushing a barge loaded with building materials, is also waiting to use the lock.

In 1983, Acaster's Water Transport bought the diesel pull-tug *Snatchette* (built by Dunstons in 1953) from Medway owners, converted it for push towing and fitted a retractable wheelhouse. The 42ft x12ft tug, renamed *Little Shifta*, is shown here in 1992 being helped by the motor barge *Kirkby* to take the dumb barge *River Star*, loaded with paper, up the Ouse to York. (H.M. Lobley)

Acasters turned *Kirkby*, visible on the previous illustration, into the push tug *Little Kirkby* after slicing off its bows. The vessel is preparing to push the dumb barge *Selby Libra*, loaded with over 200 tons of transhipped fluorspar, from Goole to Rotherham in 1999. (Mike Brown)

Above: Acasters had the 500hp push-tug *Little Shuva* purpose-built in 1996 for the weekly deliveries to York of 200 tons of rolls of Scandinavian paper from Goole. Pushing the dumb barges *River Star* and *Twite* in 1997, the tug enters the river Foss from the Ouse shortly before the end of this working, York's last regular commercial traffic.

In 1998, LASH barges returned to the Humber waterways. John Dean's tug *Lashette*, purpose-built for work with the system on the Medway, is shunting barges to and from the feeder-ship *Spruce* at Immingham. The tug and its sister vessel, *Shovette*, also now owned by Dean's Tugs, each have two 365hp Caterpillar engines driving through rotating Schottel units. The semi-submersible *Spruce* has brought eighteen dumb craft, several loaded with rice or timber from the USA, from the mother ship in Rotterdam's Europort and will return across the North Sea carrying barges loaded with British steel.

Opposite below: Negotiating the 90-degree bend in the S&SYN at Mexborough. *Little Shuva*, *Little Kirkby* and *Resilience* are bound for Goole with a large extraction column for export. *Little Kirkby* is acting as brake and bow thruster whilst *Little Shuva* provides the power for forward movement.

Above: Both *Freight Endeavour* and *Gillian Knight* were purchased by Dean's Tugs and are seen as they leave Goole's Ocean Lock for the river Ouse with LASH barges in 1998. The barges had collected scrap steel, lorried from Sheffield, for export.

After December 2002 when coal deliveries by water to Ferrybridge C Power Station ceased, Cawoods Hargreaves craft were left without work until, in mid-2003, they joined craft on the Besthorpe-Whitwood aggregate delivery run. Coamings had been fitted to some of their pans to increase their freeboard and aluminium hatch covers added for their usage on tidal rivers. *CH 109* is seen in 2004 holding pans beneath the Trentside loading staithe, with the new bow section fitted to one of the pans also visible. (Mike Brown)

Right: Hargreaves push tugs *CH 101* and *CH 108* helping out John Dean, at a time of low river levels, by pushing a LASH barge loaded with 380 tons of American rice up the river Ouse early in 2005. The photograph was taken from the new Selby bypass bridge which has, at last, eliminated the traffic delays in the town caused by the toll bridge. (Mike Brown)

Opposite below: It is now generally accepted that large indivisible loads are best carried by water, wherever possible. An example was shown on page 125 and here, Dean's Tugs' *Freight Endeavour* and the just visible bow tug *Gillian Knight* manoeuvre the barge *Landrager 19*, carrying an outsize load of a 300-ton transformer bound for Cottam Power Station, up the Trent at Gainsborough in 1998.

Other titles published by Tempus

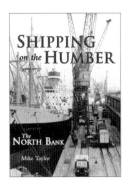

Shipping on the Humber The North Bank
MIKE TAYLOR

This fascinating collection of images depicts the entire history of shipping on the river Humber. It features many illustrations and maps, accompanied by interesting and informative text.

0 7524 3116 1

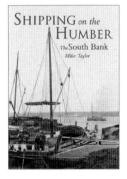

Shipping on the Humber The South Bank
MIKE TAYLOR

Mike Taylor has collated a diverse selection of material to illustrate the history of shipping on the river Humber.using a variety of images and maps. and revealing the history of the growth and decline of the industry and the area.

0 7524 2780 6

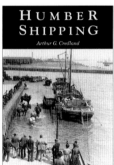

Humber Shipping
ARTHUR G. CREDLAND

Over a long period the city of Kingston upon Hull grew to be one of Britain's major ports and shipbuilding centres. But now many docks and warehouses have gone and the fishing fleet is greatly reduced. Illustrated with over 200 images, Humber Shipping reveals the changing faces of the Humber's maritime history.

0 7524 3085 8

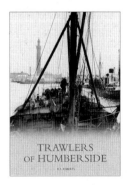

Trawlers of the Humberside
R.F. ROBERTS

Fishing in Humberside was a large and lucrative business. Illustrated with over 100 old photographs, this book reveals the concise history of each craft and the crew of many of the trawlers that sailed from Humberside, as well as reports of sinkings or other disasters.

0 7524 3167 6

If you are interested in purchasing other books published by Tempus, or in case you have difficulty finding any Tempus books in your local bookshop, you can also place orders directly through our website

www.tempus-publishing.com